STUDY GUIDES
*General Editors:* John Peck and Martin Coyle

## Palgrave Study Guides

Authoring a PhD
Career Skills
Critical Thinking Skills
e-Learning Skills
Effective Communication for
  Arts and Humanities Students
Effective Communication for
  Science and Technology
The Foundations of Research
The Good Supervisor
How to Manage your Arts, Humanities and
  Social Science Degree
How to Manage your Distance and
  Open Learning Course
How to Manage your Postgraduate Course
How to Manage your Science and
  Technology Degree
How to Study Foreign Languages
How to Write Better Essays
IT Skills for Successful Study
Making Sense of Statistics
The Mature Student's Guide to Writing
The Postgraduate Research Handbook

Presentation Skills for Students
The Principles of Writing in Psychology
Professional Writing
Research Using IT
Skills for Success
The Student Life Handbook
The Palgrave Student Planner
The Student's Guide to Writing (2nd edn)
The Study Skills Handbook (2nd edn)
Study Skills for Speakers of English as
  a Second Language
Studying the Built Environment
Studying Economics
Studying History (2nd edn)
Studying Mathematics and its Applications
Studying Modern Drama (2nd edn)
Studying Physics
Studying Programming
Studying Psychology
Teaching Study Skills and Supporting Learning
Work Placements – A Survival Guide for Students
Write it Right
Writing for Engineers (3rd edn)

## Palgrave Study Guides: Literature

*General Editors: John Peck and Martin Coyle*

How to Begin Studying English Literature
  (3rd edn)
How to Study a Jane Austen Novel (2nd edn)
How to Study a Charles Dickens Novel
How to Study Chaucer (2nd edn)
How to Study an E. M. Forster Novel
How to Study James Joyce
How to Study Linguistics (2nd edn)

How to Study Modern Poetry
How to Study a Novel (2nd edn)
How to Study a Poet (2nd edn)
How to Study a Renaissance Play
How to Study Romantic Poetry (2nd edn)
How to Study a Shakespeare Play (2nd edn)
How to Study Television
Practical Criticism

# HOW TO STUDY A POET

## John Peck

palgrave

Published by
PALGRAVE
Houndmills, Basingstoke, Hampshire RG21 6XS and
175 Fifth Avenue, New York, N. Y. 10010
Companies and representatives throughout the world

PALGRAVE is the new global academic imprint of
St. Martin's Press LLC Scholarly and Reference Division and
Palgrave Publishers Ltd (formerly Macmillan Press Ltd).

ISBN–13: 978–0–333–44262–3
ISBN–10: 0–333–44262–8

This book is printed on paper suitable for recycling and
made from fully managed and sustained forest sources.

A catalogue record for this book is available
from the British Library.

19  18  17  16  15  14

10  09  08  07  06  05

Printed in China

# Contents

# General Editors' Preface

EVERYBODY who studies literature, either for an examination or simply for pleasure, experiences the same problem: how to understand and respond to the text. As every student of literature knows, it is perfectly possible to read a book over and over again and yet still feel baffled and at a loss as to what to say about it. One answer to this problem, of course, is to accept someone else's view of the text, but how much more rewarding it would be if you could work out your own critical response to any book you choose or are required to study.

The aim of this series is to help you develop your critical skills by offering practical advice about how to read, understand and analyse literature. Each volume provides you with a clear method of study so that you can see how to set about tackling texts on your own. While the authors of each volume approach the problem in a different way, every book in the series attempts to provide you with some broad ideas about the kind of texts you are likely to be studying and some broad ideas about how to think about literature; each volume then shows you how to apply these ideas in a way which should help you construct your own analysis and interpretation. Unlike most critical books, therefore, the books in this series do not simply convey someone else's thinking about a text, but encourage you and show you how to think about a text for yourself.

Each book is written with an awareness that you are likely to be preparing for an examination, and therefore practical advice is given not only on how to understand and analyse literature, but also on how to organise a written response. Our hope is that although these books are intended to serve a practical purpose, they may also enrich your enjoyment of literature by making you a more confident reader, alert to the interest and pleasure to be derived from literary texts.

John Peck
Martin Coyle

# Acknowledgements

The author and publishers wish to thank the following who have kindly given permission for the use of copyright material:

A. P. Watt Ltd on behalf of Michael B. Yeats for two stanzas of 'The Lake Isle of Innisfree' from *The Collected Poems of W. B. Yeats* (London: Macmillan); Macmillan Publishing Company for two stanzas of 'The Lake Isle of Innisfree' from *The Poems of W. B. Yeats: A New Edition*, ed. Richard J. Finneran (New York: Macmillan, 1983).

Every effort has been made to trace all the copyright holders but if any have been inadvertently overlooked the publishers will be pleased to make the necessary arrangement at the first opportunity.

*For Alison*

# 1

## First steps

THE two poets I studied in most detail at school were John Donne and John Keats. Donne, I discovered, was a seventeenth-century clergyman who wrote difficult poems about his love of God and equally difficult poems about his love for women. They certainly were difficult poems; I am not exaggerating when I say that I did not understand any of them. I must have managed to stumble out a satisfactory examination answer on Donne, however, as I did go on to study English at university (where, I might add, Donne remained just about as much of a mystery to me as he had at school). I imagine that in the examination I must have waffled about the intensity of Donne's love, and thrown in a quotation whenever I got stuck. I might have managed to convince the examiner that I knew something about Donne, but I knew that I was totally lost with this writer.

My response to Keats, another writer new to me at the time, was far more positive. In most of the poems we studied, I could actually see what he was concerned about. My understanding might have been limited, but, compared to my understanding of Donne, my grasp of Keats was first-rate. The problems began when I had to write an essay about Keats, as I did not really know what to say about poetry. I seem to remember that my usual approach was to tell the 'story' of a poem and then say what I thought it meant, but such an approach did strike me as clumsy. I felt there must be a better way of doing it. Part of the difficulty was that I genuinely liked Keats's poetry, but did not have a method adequate to expressing my enjoyment of it.

The problems I experienced with these writers are, I think, the difficulties a lot of people experience with poetry. A great deal of poetry is hard to understand, and then, if you do understand a writer, there is the question of what to say about the poems you have read. This book tries to provide answers to these problems: it shows you how to understand a poet's works, and then shows you how to talk about his or her verse. What has to be said at the beginning of a book such as this, however, is that the suggestions offered here do not represent the only way of tackling an author. These are methods I have found useful and which I like to think some of the people I have taught have found useful. I did eventually get to understand Donne's poetry, or at least to understand it sufficiently to enable me to enjoy it, and I am no longer tongue-tied when it comes to discussing Keats. What has helped me sort out my view of these writers is the way of looking at poetry that I describe in this book. The same approach should help you with the poet or poets you are studying. It might be that the particular poet you are interested in is not referred to here, but try to see how I present an approach that should work with any poet. You might, therefore, find it useful to persevere all the way through this book, even if you are studying none of the writers discussed. That, however, is for you to decide: what follows is a method for tackling poetry which should not only help you in examinations but also, I hope, increase your understanding and enjoyment of poetry.

*Seeing what a poem is about*

Our starting-point has got to be the fact that it is possible to read a poem and have very little idea what it is about. In some cases this is because the poem is deliberately difficult, but often the problem is more basic. There are many poems that are easy to read but at the end of which you can feel at a total loss as to what they amount to. Rather than discuss the issue any further in general terms, let me provide an example: a poem by a Victorian writer, Matthew Arnold, entitled 'Dover Beach':

> The sea is calm to-night.
> The tide is full, the moon lies fair
> Upon the straits; – on the French coast the light
> Gleams and is gone; the cliffs of England stand,
> Glimmering and vast, out in the tranquil bay.
> Come to the window, sweet is the night-air!
> Only, from the long line of spray
> Where the sea meets the moon-blanch'd land,
> Listen! you hear the grating roar
> Of pebbles which the waves draw back, and fling,
> At their return, up the high strand,

Begin, and cease, and then again begin,
With tremulous cadence slow, and bring
The eternal note of sadness in.

Sophocles long ago
Heard it on the Ægæan, and it brought
Into his mind the turbid ebb and flow
Of human misery; we
Find also in the sound a thought,
Hearing it by this distant northern sea.

The Sea of Faith
Was once, too, at the full, and round earth's shore
Lay like the folds of a bright girdle furl'd;
But now I only hear
Its melancholy, long, withdrawing roar,
Retreating, to the breath
Of the night-wind, down the vast edges drear
And naked shingles of the world.

Ah, love, let us be true
To one another! for the world, which seems
To lie before us like a land of dreams,
So various, so beautiful, so new,
Hath really neither joy, nor love, nor light,
Nor certitude, nor peace, nor help for pain;
And we are here as on a darkling plain
Swept with confused alarms of struggle and flight,
Where ignorant armies clash by night.

This could be described as a fairly straightforward poem, but you
will not be alone if you soon lost any sense of its meaning. Most
readers would probably be able to grasp that the poet is in a room
at Dover looking out of the window and describing the view, but
what could prove confusing is the sudden appearance of Sophocles
and then the talk about 'The Sea of Faith'. What is the poem doing
or saying? At first it seems to be a description of the view, but at
these points it goes off in quite unexpected directions. It might be
the case, of course, that you have no difficulty in understanding
this particular poem, but I am sure you are familiar with the
problem I am describing here of finding it hard to grasp the basic
sense of a poem.

What we need is a way of confidently getting hold of this or indeed of any poem and of moving decisively beyond that first feeling of confusion. We need a method for getting at the essence of a poem, so that we can state immediately, 'This is the main thing this poem is about.' Fortunately, it is easy to grasp a poem as a whole in this way. The thing to do is to look for a contrast or opposition in the poem, a contrast which is at the heart of and which informs the whole poem. What helps in the search for this contrast is the fact that remarkably similar oppositions are at the heart of most poems. To understand this, think about life and ask yourself what the main things are that worry and distress people. I am sure that you will agree that it is things such as death and suffering, and the awareness that the lives of many people are far from happy. We worry about the state of society and about violence and cruelty, and on a more personal level we worry about the things that cause stress in our lives, such as school and work and emotional relationships. In short, we worry about a great many things all of which seem to suggest some disorder in our lives or in the world. What makes us happy is even easier to describe: we enjoy security, the security of being healthy and well-fed, of having a role in life, and relating positively to other people. We do not like to feel lost in a cruel, chaotic world; we do like to feel safe and secure in a friendly and reassuring world.

There is a sense in which every poem ever written deals with such issues. The central opposition at the heart of just about any poem is a tension between some idea of security and happiness, on the one hand, and things that are worrying, on the other. The poet confronts what can appear a baffling or frightening or depressing world and searches for something positive, something to celebrate, some sense of security. What, then, can help us with this Arnold poem, or any poem, is the confident expectation we can bring to the work that some kind of opposition on the lines described above will be at its centre. Let us see how this is the case in 'Dover Beach'. I started my discussion of the poem by saying that the speaker in his room at Dover looks out at the view. There is something secure about the narrator's position just as there is something reassuring about the calm scene he describes. As the poem goes on, however, the sea becomes turbulent and ideas come into the poem that suggest unhappiness and misery: this is particularly evident in phrases such as 'human misery' and 'we are here as on a darkling plain'. What we can say, therefore, is that the poem is built on a contrast between a sense of security and a sense of the misery of experience.

Obviously not every poem deals with the same issue as 'Dover Beach', but the point is that some such contrast between an orderly sense of experience and a disorderly sense of experience will be at the heart of most poems. Knowing this allows us to get hold of a poem very quickly; it helps us get behind the surface of a poem and see its real theme. 'Dover Beach', to return to our example, is clearly not just a piece of nature description. It is a poem about living in an insecure and frightening world, a world where, in particular, the security of religious faith has been lost. This is a big issue to explore in a short poem, but often a short poem seems weighty precisely because it is confronting these large questions about happiness and unhappiness in life. You will find it hard to grasp such matters, however, if you fail to make sensible initial moves with a poem. Begin by trying to see how a poem is built on an opposition. If you can spot a tension, between order and disorder, or between happiness and unhappiness, or between something attractive and something unattractive, then you will be well on the way towards understanding the poem.

*Building a response*

One implication of what I have been saying so far is that interpretation should start with being able to see almost at a glance what a poem is about. The secret lies in searching for a central opposition. Once you have spotted this, the poem as a whole should start to make sense quickly. In 'Dover Beach', once the sense of security and insecurity has been spotted, it is a direct journey towards realising how the poem deals with the loss of religious faith. The same will be true in the case of all poems: once you have spotted the opposition, you will only be a step away from beginning to appreciate the poem's theme.

The usefulness of the idea of an opposition does not stop at this point, however, for it can help us organise our discussion of every aspect of a poem's structure and use of language. To illustrate this, let us return to 'Dover Beach', and start with the fact that some parts of the poem suggest security whereas other parts convey a sense of insecurity. The simplest way in which this is evident is that the poem opens with some very neat sentences, with lines breaking neatly into two balanced halves; the symmetry of this is orderly and reassuring. As the poem goes on, however, the sentences become more complicated and involved, and this suggests the loss of simple convictions in life. In every poem there will be similar impressions of simplicity and lack of simplicity in the form of the verse, and it will always be the case that simple, straightforward lines will seem positive whereas complicated sentences will suggest the disorder of experience. A sense of an opposition will therefore provide a way of organising a discussion of the overall formal structure of a poem. That opposition will, however, have to resolve itself or be reconsidered before the end of the poem. This is a fundamental aspect of the structure of poetry. A theme is set up, which is built on an opposition, but for the poem to end it will need to have progressed somewhere, and this can only be done by some alteration of or fresh way of looking at the original tension.

Let me illustrate how this works in 'Dover Beach'. I have already identified a tension in the poem, how feelings of security give way to feelings of insecurity, but Arnold is unlikely to spend the whole poem in an endless moan. The poem has to arrive somewhere. Look, therefore, at the last stanza, where he pleads with his love that they be true to each other. Can you see how the poem arrives at a kind of answer, setting up love as a thing of tremendous importance in a threatening world? Clearly, the particular resolution used by Arnold will not be used by all poets, but a similar general pattern will be evident in all poems. There will always be an opposition, which should prove easy to spot as it will be dealing with some of the major things that concern us in life. If you can spot the opposition, you should then be looking for how the poet alters the balance of things as the poem approaches its end. The 'problem' in the poem will not always be resolved, of course, and sometimes, as is the case in 'Dover Beach', the ending might be rather more complicated than it initially appears to be. What leads me to say this about the ending of Arnold's poem is that he seems to know that the love he talks about is illusory, for he talks about a world that has no 'joy, nor love, nor light . . . '. Love, therefore, is dismissed as an illusion, but can you see how Arnold would rather cling to an illusion than accept a terrifying and vicious world?

What we have seen so far is how the sense of an opposition helps us over any initial feelings of confusion with a poem, bringing us very quickly to an appreciation of a poem's theme, and how it provides us with a way of describing the formal pattern of a work right through to its conclusion. The usefulness of the concept of an opposition goes further still, however, for it provides an organising framework for exploring the words out of which the poet builds his poem. I am not going to go into this in detail here, as how to talk about the language of poetry is the central subject of this book, but I will touch on one aspect of 'Dover Beach', Arnold's use of 'light' and 'dark' imagery. At the beginning of the poem, when the scene is tranquil, Arnold uses phrases such as 'the light gleams' and talks about the 'glimmering' cliffs, words which help create a sense of well-being, but by the end of the poem there is only the 'darkling plain' and the armies that 'clash by night'. The obvious point is that these 'light' and 'dark' images have helped Arnold bring his theme to life, the original opposition we noted being reflected in the use of opposing images. Wherever you look in poetry you will find that the same thing is true, that the poet uses opposing images to help realise his theme. What this means, is that, once you have spotted an opposition in a poem, the basic discussion of the poet's use of language can be quite simple, as all you need to do is spot the opposing images the writer uses and how they reflect the poem's theme.

## A further example

These brief comments about imagery anticipate areas that I do not really want to get into in this chapter, where I am only concerned to show how it is possible to get started on a poem. As I am sure is clear by now, the initial move to take with a poem is very simple indeed: it comes down to spotting an opposition and letting everything develop from there. To illustrate how this approach will work with any poem let us look now at a sonnet by William Shakespeare:

When I have seen my Time's fell hand defac'd
The rich proud cost of outworn buried age;
When sometime lofty towers I see down raz'd,
And brass eternal slave to mortal rage;
When I have seen the hungry ocean gain
Advantage on the kingdom of the shore,
And the firm soil win of the watery main,
Increasing store with loss and loss with store:
When I have seen such interchange of state,

Or state itself confounded to decay,
Ruin hath taught me thus to ruminate –
That Time will come and take my love away.
   This thought is as a death, which cannot choose
   But weep to have that which it fears to lose.

This is a difficult poem to follow, more difficult than 'Dover Beach', and is so because of the extraordinary compression of ideas throughout its fourteen lines. There is a great deal to take in, a whole series of puzzling lines. You might be able to see that it is in some way about 'Time', but have very little idea what it is saying about this subject. If a poem does puzzle you, the best way to get started is always by looking for a central opposition. Ask yourself, are there ideas and pictures in the poem that seem unattractive, and are there ideas and pictures that seem attractive? My first impression of this poem is that there is very little that is positive. It seems negative most of the time because it is packed with images of destruction and things changing and wasting away. A lot of these images are complex and difficult to absorb, but in the early stages of an analysis you can look through, and ignore, the details. Do not get trapped by every little local difficulty. Try to get at the big theme. In this poem it seems to be time as a destroyer. The idea in itself, however, is a bit flimsy unless we can find something to set against it, so we need to search for an alternative idea that is also present in the poem. The main thing I can see that Shakespeare might be offering as a positive alternative to a world of waste is the concept of love, for what distresses him most of all is that time will take his love away. In this poem, then, as in any poem, we can point to a central opposition; it is built on the idea of the attractiveness of love versus the destructive force of time.

As with many short poems, the apparent subject might be small, just the poet talking about his love, but the significance seems larger because the poem talks about what we cling on to in a world where things are for ever falling into decay. It is the images Shakespeare includes, which touch on and refer to various aspects of experience, which enable such a short poem to appear to be saying so much about life in general. For the moment, however, I do not want to go into this in any more depth. Instead, I want to concentrate on how the poem concludes; we can see that Shakespeare has set up an opposition, but the poem also needs to develop and arrive somewhere. It does not necessarily need to resolve the tension, but does need a fresh twist or direction at the end. Look again at the conclusion of the poem; do you feel that there is anything different about the last two lines? What strikes me is that Shakespeare drops his elaborate images about the effects of time and talks in a far more direct way about how the thought of losing his loved one distresses him. What has happened is that he has changed emphasis or direction to conclude his poem. There is a pleasure for us as readers, a pleasure we should be able to derive from all poems, of seeing not only how the poet sets up an opposition but also how he brings things to a fresh or original conclusion so that we look at life in a slightly new way.

*Is it really as simple as this?*

With a bit of practice, you will find it easy to spot the overall pattern in a poem, to see what opposition is set up and how the poet develops that opposition, so that he or she finally arrives at a point that is significantly different from the point at which the poem started. But is it really as simple as this? Are all poems really so similar in terms of their general themes?

My first response to this is to say that the whole issue is even more straightforward than I have suggested so far. I have used a number of terms in talking about the central thematic concerns in poetry, but it can be argued that all poetry is about love and death, and that love and death are at the centre of every great poem ever written. The reason is that we live in a world where the ultimate problem is death; the only thing we can all be sure of is that some day we shall die. That thought is chilling. We therefore need something to make life meaningful. One positive force is the love of God, but another is human love: the point is that love offers a sense of something positive that we can set against the negative fact of death. It can, therefore, be argued that the opposition at the heart of any good poem is between death and love, that the writer examines the only positive thing we have to hang on to in a potentially meaningless and death-dominated world.

Clearly, however, it would be absurdly reductive just to say about every poem that it is about love and death. That would not begin to do justice to the unique quality of every good poem. And that is the real point about the whole method I am presenting in this book. My central concern in the subsequent chapters is with how poets fill out their basic patterns. Grasping a central opposition only provides you with a beginning, an initial secure hold on the poem which can provide a solid foundation for your subsequent comments. Where so many examination candidates go wrong, however, is that they never get hold of this basic picture, so find themselves lost in a maze, unable to see the broad pattern. It is therefore vital to start by getting hold of the poem as a whole, but this leads on to looking at what really makes a poem come to life, which, as my subsequent chapters explain, is the poet's use of language. What we have done so far is comparable to saying that London and Tokyo are large cities: we have seen the ground-plan that underlies poems, but we have not yet begun to talk about the real texture of individual poems and specific poets. That kind of exploration of the verse itself becomes central in the next chapter, but there are a few more general points that are perhaps best made here.

## Getting the measure of a poet

Thematically most poems have a lot in common, but the way in which every poet uses language to develop his or her theme makes every poem unique. Not only does an individual poem have a character of its own, however; the works of a poet represent his or her unique poetic voice. He or she is saying things that nobody else has ever said. This book deals with how to pursue that sense of a poet; its aim is not so much to help you discuss individual poems as to help you piece together a view of an author. And, as you might have guessed from what I have said so far, I am going to suggest that the most rewarding approach is to build that view from the evidence of the poems themselves. Indeed, could there be an approach other than reading and thinking about the poems and thereby eventually arriving at your view of the poet?

The sad fact is, however, that most students most of the time do not approach a poet through the poetry itself. So what do they do instead? Often they approach the poetry from the outside, perhaps through facts about the poet's life and times. I am not saying these facts are unimportant, but it must be clear that they should take second place to a consideration of the actual words of the poems themselves. In the same way, a look at the verse itself should always precede any sense of the poet's ideas or 'philosophy'. In marking exam papers it is sometimes apparent that the candidates are familiar with the poet's views, but write about the ideas with only incidental references to the poetry. They might, for example, say that the poet believed in this or that idea, and then say that this can be seen in a certain poem, which is only referred to by its title. Can you see how this downgrades the verse and makes it secondary, as if the poet's ideas are more important than his or her actual writing? My point is that everything should come from the poetry itself, so even if you are writing about the poet's ideas you should attempt to show how his or her ideas can be established from the evidence of specific poems.

### Putting the poetry first

If this seems a bit daunting, I am sure that light will dawn as the rest of this book shows you how to talk about poetry. The reason why students shy away from close attention to poems is that working just from the words on the page seems difficult. You cannot surround yourself with information and bolster up your argument with solid facts; it is just you and the poems, and the difficult challenge of talking about writing. But this is the only way to do it, and, as I hope to show, it is not that difficult, and certainly enjoyable. I have tried to keep true to my own principles throughout this book, wherever possible avoiding assertions about writers in advance of looking at specific poems and always trying to build my entire view from the poetry itself.

This is the most sensible way to work, and will serve you well in examinations. Examination questions about poetry are very straightforward. Almost invariably you will be asked to offer your view of the concerns and nature of a writer's work. The secret of producing a good answer lies in how you tackle the question. If you rush in and produce a general account of what the author's poems are about, then your answer will be poor. If, however, you work from short extracts, building a sense of what the poet is like, then your answer will do justice to both the themes and the texture of the verse. You will find yourself building a convincing case, solidly based on the evidence. But there are other matters that will concern you at the beginning, in particular how to set about reading a poet.

### The first reading

It is impossible to tell you how to read, as opposed to how to study, an author, as people like to read in different ways and at different speeds. If I had to study a poet, though, I would start by reading a sizable selection of his or her works fairly quickly. I would read through the poems two or three times, in a fairly casual, almost lazy way, not worrying too much about what they all amounted to. I would try to be a sponge, soaking up the writer, getting the feel of his or her work even though I might not have the words to describe my impressions. You might, of course, find it hard to read a poet in this way; you might find that your concentration wavers, and that it wavers even during the reading of a single poem. If this is the case, you need not feel guilty about it. The literary works which most hold our attention are those that tell a story, where we become engrossed in the narrative. Most poems, however, do not tell a story, and it is this more than anything else that affects our concentration. One approach that can help is if, even on this first reading, you employ the approach I have described of searching for a central opposition. At that point, the poem, and your mind, will cease to wander as you seek a shape and direction in the work.

After my initial reading, I would try to write down any ideas, however piecemeal, that I had formed about the poet. These words might well prove to be the words I am searching for when I actually start to analyse the author's works. Often, however, I might have absolutely nothing to say about my general impressions, so it is at this point that I would start working on an individual poem. Just what 'work' on a poem involves should become clear in the following chapters, but I want to end this one with a quick recapitulation of the first steps it is possible to take with a poem.

*Getting hold of a poem: two further examples*

I have talked about the frequency with which love is offered as an alternative to death in poetry, but my two examples so far have concentrated on human love. What I want to look at here is a poem that is clearly religious, primarily to show how this tension can operate in a religious work. The poem is John Milton's 'On his Blindness':

When I consider how my light is spent,
  E're half my days, in this dark world and wide,
  And that one Talent, which is death to hide,
  Lodg'd with me useless, though my soul more bent

To serve therewith my Maker, and present
  My true account, lest he returning chide,
  Doth God exact day-labour, light deny'd
  I fondly ask; But patience to prevent
That murmer, soon replies, God doth not need
  Either men's work or his own gifts, who best
  Bear his milde yoak, they serve him best, his State
Is Kingly. Thousands at his bidding speed
  And post o're Land and Ocean without rest:
  They also serve who only stand and waite.

I should imagine that you soon got lost in the immensely long
opening sentence of this poem, but do not assume that this means
that you have necessarily failed to understand the poem. If Milton
has written an intricate and difficult sentence in which it is difficult
to follow the meaning, might not the sentence be telling us through
the very complications of form what it is like to live in a bewildering
world? I certainly cannot understand every image and fresh twist
in this sentence at first glance, but I can pick up and comment on
some lines that do seem to make immediate sense. The first two
lines are

  When I consider how my light is spent,
  E're half my days, in this dark world and wide . . . .

We know that the subject of the poem is Milton's blindness, but
these lines seem to have a greater weight of meaning than that, for
they speak for us all when they talk about the feeling of being lost
in a dark world. The rest of the opening sentence, it can be
assumed, develops Milton's description of his feelings of despair as
a blind man, but probably also carries a more general meaning
about mankind's feelings of inadequacy and confusion in a baffling
world.

  What we have seen so far is how the structure of a sentence and
the words used can create one side of the opposition in a poem. For
the poem to work, though, something has to be set against this, and
surely this becomes apparent in the second half of the poem. The
sentences become shorter, simpler and more confident, and the
images are less difficult to understand. What Milton is now talking
about is a simple and happy relationship with God. The overall
opposition in the poem, therefore, is immensely simple: on the one

hand, a picture of being lost in a dark and troubling world, but, on the other hand, God's love flooding into the poem as a positive alternative. That simple, confident trust in God is summed up in the concluding one-line aphorism: 'They also serve who only stand and waite'. The brevity and memorability of the line suggests that the poet has conquered all feelings of despair and can sum up a central truth of experience in a line. It is, then, a poem built on a simple opposition, but, as should be apparent in these comments I have made about it, criticism really begins when, having spotted the opposition, you look at how the poet handles the structure and language of his poem to bring his ideas to life.

The first and vital move, however, is looking for an opposition and thereby trying to get hold of the work as a whole. This will often involve trying to look through the surface difficulty of a poem. But what also has to be admitted is that the problem with some poems is not that they are difficult but that they are uninteresting. Or, at least, superficially uninteresting. I am sure you have read a great many poems which have entirely failed to capture your attention, where your response has been closer to a yawn than to intellectual confusion. I remember one examination I took where we had to discuss a poem by a writer called Edwin Arlington Robinson. The poem did nothing at all for me. I read it carefully, but I did not have any views about it and could not think of anything to say about it. I could not really tell the examiner that I thought it was a boring little poem that was not worth reading, so I imagine that I must have adopted my standard, if somewhat clumsy, approach of more or less summarising the poem and then adding a few dishonest comments about it being an interesting work. I have never looked at this poem since that examination, so it might be a good idea to examine it here to see if the approach of looking for a central opposition allows me to organise a more worthwhile response:

> No more with overflowing light
> Shall fill the eyes that now are faded,
> Nor shall another's fringe with night
> Their woman-hidden world as they did.
> No more shall quiver down the days
> The flowing wonder of her ways,
> Whereof no language may requite
> The shifting and the many-shaded.

The grace, divine, definitive
Clings only as a faint forestalling;
The laugh that love could not forgive
Is hushed, and answers to no calling;
The forehead and the little ears
Have gone where Saturn keeps the years;
The breast where roses could not live
Has done with rising and with falling.

The beauty, shattered by the laws
That have creation in their keeping,
No longer trembles at applause,
Or over children that are sleeping;
And we who delve in beauty's lore
Know all that we have known before
Of what inexorable cause
Makes time so vicious in his reaping.

Reading through the poem, I can recall the clumsiness of my original analysis, when I must have said that the poem is about a dead woman, and then gone through it more or less rephrasing or interpreting every line.

How much more confident it would have been to say that the subject of the poem is a dead woman, but the poem works on the basis of setting the fact of her death against the memory of how she was when she was alive. This gives me a framework for organising my comments about everything that I find in the poem. Essentially this would involve spotting negative and positive details in the poem, and seeing how they are set against each other. The poem starts, for example, with the negative 'No more . . . ', and this side of things is maintained with a word such as 'faded', in the second line. But what we also have to note is how positive images are used to create a sense of life: this is apparent in 'overflowing light' at the outset, and is then maintained in images which suggest a sense of somebody physically present yet delicate. This is seen in the references to her laugh, her forehead, and her little ears in the second stanza. The whole poem is built on an opposition between this sense of life and loveliness as against the heavy fact of death.

Can you see how finding an opposition at the heart of the poem immediately gives a shape and direction to all my comments? I am no longer in the awkward position of just saying 'This phrase is interesting' or 'This is a good choice of word.' Instead, I can always say how an attractive image creates the sense of the woman alive, and how this is played off against ideas of destruction and loss. My analysis would involve looking at many more of the details of the poem, but essentially I would be talking about how the details of the poem bring the theme to life. The other thing I need to do, however, is to look at where this poem, or any poem, arrives. As I have said already, there is likely to be a fresh twist or new angle at the end. At the end of this poem, for example, the poet shifts from the dead lady to those of us who live on. What he in effect says is that we all already know about the cruel destructiveness of time. It is as if he acknowledges how poets always write on familiar themes, but also how his poem has managed to make us look anew at an old theme. The central way in which it achieves this is through the power of the poet's language in suggesting both the vicious destructiveness of time and death, and the fragile, delicate beauty of the one who has been destroyed.

I hope it is apparent again how simple the initial moves with a poem can, perhaps indeed should, be. It is a case of looking for the central opposition, taking a brief look at how the details start to bring the opposition to life, and seeing where the poem arrives. If your reading of an individual poem is built on the basis of these simple foundations, then you can be reasonably confident that your final, overall reading of a writer will be very impressive indeed. How to build that reading and take your first view further is the subject of the next and subsequent chapters.

# 2

## The interpretation of poetry

IN this chapter I deal with how you can construct a full analysis of a poem and how analyses of individual poems can be put together to build a view of a writer. As always, I am going to deal with specific examples – in this chapter, poems by John Keats and Wilfred Owen – but I hope it is clear that the strategies I describe should work with any writer. More often than not, when you have to study a poet you are likely to be encountering his or her works for the first time, so let us start from that position. You have just discovered that you have to look at the poetry of John Keats. Where and how do you begin?

### John Keats

As a first step you should read through a selection of Keats's poems. The position in which you might find yourself is that you do not really know what to think; the poems seem interesting at times, but no coherent view develops in your mind. I hope you will not be insulted if I suggest that the best thing to do is to read the poems again: there is no substitute for reading and rereading an author. It is clear to every examiner that the candidates who do best are those who know the books best. If a view still stubbornly refuses to form, however, do not let it worry you. Some ideas will quickly begin to take shape as soon as you look closely at an individual poem. But there is still the problem of where to begin. How do you select a poem for discussion? How do you know that the poem you have chosen is worth considering? There are, I think, two answers to these questions: if you have got a lot of confidence, look at one of the poems you most liked. Alternatively, rely on someone else's guidance, perhaps by seeing what poems by your writer are included in an anthology of English poetry.

The poem I am going to start with is one of Keats's most

famous, and therefore most frequently anthologised, poems, his
**'Ode to a Nightingale'**. It is a fairly long poem, but it should
make the rest of this chapter clearer if I give it in full here:

My heart aches, and a drowsy numbness pains
   My sense, as though of hemlock I had drunk,
Or emptied some dull opiate to the drains
   One minute past, and Lethe-wards had sunk:
'Tis not through envy of thy happy lot,
   But being too happy in thine happiness, –
      That thou, light-winged Dryad of the trees,
        In some melodious plot
   Of beeches green, and shadows numberless,
      Singest of summer in full-throated ease.

O, for a draught of vintage! that hath been
   Cool'd a long age in the deep-delved earth,
Tasting of Flora and the country green,
   Dance, and Provençal song, and sunburnt mirth!
O for a beaker full of the warm South,
   Full of the true, the blushful Hippocrene,
      With beaded bubbles winking at the brim,
        And purple-stained mouth;
   That I might drink, and leave the world unseen,
      And with thee fade away into the forest dim:

Fade far away, dissolve, and quite forget
   What thou among the leaves hast never known,
The weariness, the fever, and the fret
   Here, where men sit and hear each other groan;
Where palsy shakes a few, sad, last gray hairs,
   Where youth grows pale, and spectre-thin, and dies;
      Where but to think is to be full of sorrow
        And leaden-eyed despairs,
   Where Beauty cannot keep her lustrous eyes,
      Or new Love pine at them beyond to-morrow.

Away! away! for I will fly to thee,
   Not charioted by Bacchus and his pards,
But on the viewless wings of Poesy,
   Though the full brain perplexes and retards:

Already with thee! tender is the night,
  And haply the Queen-Moon is on her throne,
    Cluster'd around by all her starry Fays;
      But here there is no light,
  Save what from heaven is with the breezes blown
    Through verdurous glooms and winding mossy ways.

I cannot see what flowers are at my feet,
  Nor what soft incense hangs upon the boughs,
But, in embalmed darkness, guess each sweet
  Wherewith the seasonable month endows
The grass, the thicket, and the fruit-tree wild;
  White hawthorn, and the pastoral eglantine;
    Fast fading violets cover'd up in leaves;
      And mid-May's eldest child,
  The coming musk-rose, full of dewy wine,
    The murmurous haunt of flies on summer eves.

Darkling I listen; and, for many a time
  I have been half in love with easeful Death,
Call'd him soft names in many a mused rhyme,
  To take into the air my quiet breath;
Now more than ever seems it rich to die,
  To cease upon the midnight with no pain,
    While thou art pouring forth thy soul abroad
      In such an ecstasy!
  Still wouldst thou sing, and I have ears in vain –
    To thy high requiem become a sod.

Thou wast not born for death, immortal Bird!
  No hungry generations tread thee down;
The voice I hear this passing night was heard
  In ancient days by emperor and clown:
Perhaps the self-same song that found a path
  Through the sad heart of Ruth, when, sick for home,
    She stood in tears amid the alien corn;
      The same that oft-times hath
  Charm'd magic casements, opening on the foam
    Of perilous seas, in faery lands forlorn.

Forlorn! the very word is like a bell
  To toll me back from thee to my sole self!
Adieu! the fancy cannot cheat so well
  As she is fam'd to do, deceiving elf.
Adieu! adieu! thy plaintive anthem fades
  Past the near meadows, over the still stream,
    Up the hill-side; and now 'tis buried deep
      In the next valley-glades:
Was it a vision, or a waking dream?
  Fled is that music: – Do I wake or sleep?

Start by reading the poem slowly and carefully. It might be that
this careful reading of 'Ode to a Nightingale' generates all kinds of
ideas, but it is far more likely that you will simply feel at a loss. It
could well be that all you can find to say at this stage is that this is
a poem about a nightingale.

We are stuck then. Where do we go from here? As it is a fairly
long poem, the logical thing to do would seem to be to look closely
at its opening. I have decided to look at the whole of the opening
stanza, and what I hope to find, even this early, are some
indications of a central opposition, which should help me grasp the
true subject of the poem. This is the first step:

1   *Look for a central opposition in the poem*

In the first stanza of 'Ode to a Nightingale', Keats describes how
he feels and then goes on to mention a nightingale. I need to find a
tension or opposition in the stanza, and what can help me is the
knowledge that time and time again in poems an idea of something
pleasant or attractive will be set against an idea of something
unpleasant. The poem beings,

My heart aches, and a drowsy numbness pains
  My sense, as though of hemlock I had drunk . . . .

The words 'my heart aches' and the reference to pain suggest the
poet's unhappiness, but by the end of the stanza everything seems
pleasant. There is something very relaxed and happy about the
nightingale who 'Singest of summer in full-throated ease'. I can
now sum up the opposition in the poem in a very simple way: a
sense of 'pain' is set against an impression of 'ease'. The poet is

contrasting his own depressed feelings with the joy represented by the nightingale. As he continues, Keats is likely to build upon and explore this tension.

The point we have arrived at now is that a look at just one stanza has already led to a clear view of the central opposition in the poem. You might be wondering whether analysis of poetry can really be as straightforward as this. Is it legitimate to start making sense of a poem in this almost ruthlessly methodical way? The point is, however, that appreciation of the marvellous way in which Keats brings his theme to life must start with a clear grasp of the theme. You need to recognise very quickly how a poet deals with common problems in life so that you have a foundation for discussing fully his original treatment of familiar issues. And the familiar issue here seems to be, on the basis of the evidence examined so far, the tension between the pain the poet experiences and a vision of happiness that transcends everyday experience.

Once you have identified the theme in a poem, the next step is to start looking at how the poet presents and develops his central opposition:

2   *Begin to look at the details of the poem, trying to see how the poet brings his theme to life*

It would be possible to stick with this first stanza, exploring the significance of the particular words Keats uses, but as this is a long poem it seems more sensible to move on. I have identified an opposition, so the best approach is to look for lines in the poem where he develops the picture of joy and also lines where he talks again about his unhappy feelings. The opening of the second stanza seems promising:

> O for a draught of vintage! that hath been
>   Cool'd a long age in the deep-delved earth,
> Tastings of Flora and the country green,
>   Dance, and Provençal song, and sunburnt mirth!

Selecting a few lines for close discussion means that my comments about the poem are going to be precise rather than too generalised. It is always wise to pick a few lines for analysis rather than just summarising the general drift of one or more stanzas. You do have to be very conscious of what you are doing, however, when you start to focus closely. The most common mistake is to pick out words or phrases and more or less just say, 'That's interesting' or 'That's nice.' What you have to bear in mind all the time is that you are interested in how the words and phrases enable the poet to realise his theme. When you pick out something for discussion, therefore, you must always make sure that you explain what it contributes and how it contributes to the poem as a whole. That is easy to do, however, as you already have a sense of the poem's broad theme, so the justification of the details you select for scrutiny will always be that they bring this theme to life.

We can start with the first word, 'O'. If we bear in mind that Keats's concern in the poem is with the world of the nightingale and how this transcends the pain of dull reality, then we should be able to see how the initial 'O' signals to us that he is leaving behind the real world for the world he longs for. The words that follow create a picture of a happy world of the senses. In discussing lines such as these, do not make the mistake of concentrating too much on the sounds of the words. That can lead you into the trap of ascribing all kinds of mysterious qualities to certain sounds. Sound is important in poetry, but get your priorities right: the central thing is the meaning of the words and what the words suggest. There are several things that strike one in these lines: one is that it is an attractive world of the senses, where we can taste and feel its pleasures. And when Keats talks about the 'earth' and the 'country green' we feel that we are being presented with the most pleasant face of nature. Yet the references to 'Flora' and 'Provençal song' just serve to distance it a bit from any familiar English landscape, and so invest the poet's imagined world with rather special qualities. Yet, if it is a dream world he describes, it is a very tangible one, a firm and substantial world that delights the senses. Now it might be that you spot very different things in these lines, but that is how it should be. I have merely offered my impression of how the lines work to create a certain effect. You might pick up different details and have different ideas about the effect they create, but the all-important thing is to do as I have tried to do here, and make that connection between the particular details and the larger theme you have already perceived in the poem.

The positive power of these few lines should become even more apparent when we contrast them with a 'negative' section from the poem. I looked around for some lines where Keats returns to and

develops his picture of the world of 'pain', and selected this passage
from the third stanza:

> Here, where men sit and hear each other groan;
> Where palsy shakes a few, sad, last gray hairs,
>   Where youth grows pale, and spectre-thin, and dies . . . .

Here is an unrelenting sequence of unhappy and painful images.
These lines convey the harsh reality of this world where pain,
suffering and death exist, and obviously contrast sharply with the
joyous passages in the poem. But we can be far more precise about
the specific method Keats employs. The simple fact is that, in order
to convey this 'negative' impression, he selects images which are
the exact opposite of his happy images. His happy vision was
characterised by the strong colour of 'country green', but here the
word chosen is 'pale'. 'Spectre-thin' has replaced that earlier sense
of solid substantiality. The joyous sound of 'Provençal song' has
yielded to groans. And the general impression of this 'real' world is
rather ghostly and nightmarish; whereas the imagined world
seemed concrete and substantial. One of the particular effects of
this poem, then, is that the imagined world begins to seem not only
preferable to but almost more real than the world in which Keats
actually lives, but what should also be clear here is the point about
how a poet handles images. A poem is built on an opposition, and
this opposition operates throughout and at every level in the poem.
In all writers you will find that one group of images is set against
opposing images, this clash enabling the poet to fill out, develop and
bring his theme to life in a forceful and memorable way. Your
analysis of a poem will therefore come to life as you look at some of
these ways in which the poet uses details to develop this basic
opposition.

   In fact, this analysis of the details at various stages of the poem
could go on and on, as there is just such a concentrated use of
language in poetry, but rather than labour the point it is always
wise to focus on just a couple of small areas of the text, trying to
establish as much as you can from this small amount of evidence.
Such close attention to just two passages will enable you to say
something very precise about the poem and yet also enable you to
offer a strong, developing sense of the poem as a whole. And, as
your sense of the poem develops, what you will need to look at next

is how the poem does actually develop. You need to look for sigrs of progress in the poem – that is, for evidence of how the poet is developing or complicating his theme. This can become the third step in an analytic method:

3   *Look at another section of the poem, trying to see how the poem is progressing*

All that is involved in poetry criticism is seeing what a poem is about, and then looking at how the poet brings his or her theme to life. As you do this, you will find yourself adding to your overall sense of what the poem is about. As the poem continues, a more and more complex picture will be developing. In order to track the poem's development, it is a good idea to select a passage about two-thirds of the way through the work for discussion. You might, subsequently, want to return and explore every change of course in the poem, but rather than getting trapped in too much detail it is sensible to keep moving forward, picking selected sections for analysis. As I say, you can be confident that by about two-thirds of the way through some interesting development will be taking place. With a short poem, such as a sonnet, I would focus on what is happening around the ninth to twelfth lines, but in the case of 'Ode to a Nightingale' I have decided to have a closer look at the fifth of its eight stanzas.

Remember that Keats is contrasting the painful real world and a world of 'ease', and in this fifth stanza he again seems to be creating a picture of that happier world as he describes a rich world of nature:

> White hawthorn, and the postoral eglantine;
>    Fast fading violets covered up in leaves;
>       And mid-May's eldest child,
> The coming musk-rose, full of dewy wine,
>    The murmurous haunt of flies on summer eves.

The simplest way of coming to terms with any passage is to ask yourself whether the impression created is attractive or unattractive. Does the poet seem happy or ill at ease in some way? At first sight everything does seem splendid here. It is vivid and substantial, with its references to particular plants such as the 'White hawthorn', and there is a lush richness in a phrase such as 'full of dewy wine'.

These images add to the poem's sense of a world of natural abundance which is at such odds with this world 'Where youth grows pale, and spectre-thin, and dies . . . . Yet my impression is that there is something just a little bit disturbing about these lines. There is a sense of time passing in the 'Fast fading violets', as if the idea of change and decay insinuates itself even into the poet's ecstatic reverie. Most disturbing, however, is the last line, 'The murmurous haunt of flies on summer eves'. The impression as a whole is rather uncomfortable, and in particular 'murmurous' seems closer to the groaning referred to earlier in the poem than to 'Provençal song'. It is as if Keats has set his awareness of the real world against his vision of a better world in nature and the imagination, but thoughts of the real world always keep drifting back in. Painful reality keeps on disrupting his dream: what is so impressive in these lines, then, is the delicacy with which Keats undermines the more harmonious vision.

What we can see here is an interesting way in which Keats is maintaining and exploring the tension at the heart of his poem. It helps to know that the kind of way in which the tension is being handled here is a common feature in a great many poems. Many poems set up an opposition between the way things are and a vision of how they might be, and then establish a wavering balance between the two. We are attracted by the vision such poems offer of a world characterised by happiness and order, yet the strength in such poems is that they simultaneously manage to acknowledge the pain of reality. In such poems, and as is vividly the case in 'Ode to a Nightingale', the poet sets up his initial opposition, and then, as is the case here, explores the relationship between the two sides of his opposition. We should be able to see this again at the end of the poem as we

4   *Look at how the poem concludes*

A poem needs to arrive somewhere. The poet has set up an opposition, and needs to provide some final reflection on it at the end. He does not, however, need to resolve the dilemma he has explored in his poem. This should become clear in the closing words of 'Ode to a Nightingale':

> Was it a vision, or a waking dream?
>   Fled is that music: – Do I wake or sleep?

The poem ends in confusion. The vision of a better world has been so strong that Keats is tempted to think that it might really exist. But the use of two questions at the end suggests his uncertainty. We come back from a world of 'ease' to a mind which is obviously ill at ease.

5    *Sum up your sense of the poem as a whole, and your sense of the writer so far*

One of the most common misconceptions about poetry is that the poet has a 'message', that he is perhaps putting forward a simple lesson about what we should believe in or how we should behave. The kind of way in which it is possible to go wrong with 'Ode to a Nightingale' is if you cling to the idea that Keats must be 'saying' something definite, that he must be putting forward an argument. But most poetry is not as conclusive as that. What it generally does, as in 'Ode to a Nightingale', is set up a tension and explore that tension. The poet explores the relationship between our desire for a happier life and the hard facts of so much of experience. But he has no way out of the dilemma; he is reminding us of this tension that operates in all our lives. Nor need he be saying anything very new; what he can do, however, is give us a new sense, through the power of his poem, of the issues that have always concerned mankind.

At the end of a poem, therefore, in order to move towards a sense of the unique qualities of a particular writer, we need to pull back and sum up what we have learnt about the way in which the poem and this poet strike a distinctive note. The most practical approach is to write down a few simple statements saying what you can now say about this writer that you could not have said before looking at this particular poem. In the case of Keats, I feel that I have learnt four things from 'Ode to a Nightingale'.

(i)    He deals with the pain of reality and how desirable it would be to escape to a happier world.

(ii)    What is so attractive about his poetry is the vivid way in which he can create a picture of a world of the senses.

(iii)    His poem is not escapist, however. There is a clear way in which reality in his verse intermingles with and disrupts the perfect vision.

(iv)    This makes for an interesting instability in his poem, so that we are presented with a dream world but never lose sight of the real world.

No doubt there is more that could be added, and you might produce a different set of conclusions at this stage, but the important thing is that you do try to sum up at this stage. Your close attention to small sections of the poem will only really have any purpose if you pull back and try to make larger judgements along the way. It is a process that must be continued as you look at more poems by the author, going in close for discussion of the texture of his verse, but then pulling out and spelling out what you have learnt from your close focusing. The other thing that you need to remember as you look at more poems, and generally speaking a look at somewhere between three and six poems should be sufficient, is that, in order to build a view of the writer, you must try to build on what you have established so far.

In the following analysis of **'Ode on a Grecian Urn'**, therefore, try to see how the same analytic method is being employed again, but also try to see how I am attempting to add to my overall impression of Keats so far. On this occasion, however, after quoting the poem, I shall comment less on the method of the analysis and hope that, by this stage of this chapter, the illustrative reading will speak for itself:

Thou still unravish'd bride of quietness,
　　Thou foster-child of silence and slow time,
Sylvan historian, who canst thus express
　　A flowery tale more sweetly than our rhyme:
What leaf-fring'd legend haunts about they shape
　　Of deities or mortals, or of both,
　　　In Tempe or the dales of Arcady?
　　What men or gods are these? What maidens loth?
What mad pursuit? What struggle to escape?
　　　What pipes and timbrels? What wild ecstasy?

Heard melodies are sweet, but those unheard
　　Are sweeter; therefore, ye soft pipes, play on;
Not to the sensual ear, but, more endear'd,
　　Pipe to the spirit ditties of no tone:

Fair youth, beneath the trees, thou canst not leave
  Thy song, nor ever can those trees be bare;
    Bold Lover, never, never canst thou kiss,
Though winning near the goal – yet, do not grieve;
    She cannot fade, though thou has not thy bliss,
    For ever wilt thou love, and she be fair!

Ah, happy, happy boughs! that cannot shed
  Your leaves, nor ever bid the Spring adieu;
And, happy melodist, unwearied,
  For ever piping songs for ever new;
More happy love! more happy, happy love!
  For ever warm and still to be enjoy'd,
    For ever panting, and for ever young;
All breathing human passion far above,
    That leaves a heart high-sorrowful and cloy'd,
    A burning forehead, and a parching tongue.

Who are these coming to the sacrifice?
  To what green altar, O mysterious priest,
Lead'st thou that heifer lowing at the skies,
  And all her silken flanks with garlands drest?
What little town by river or sea shore,
  Or mountain-built with peaceful citadel,
    Is emptied of this folk, this pious morn?
And, little town, thy streets for evermore
  Will silent be; and not a soul to tell
    Why thou are desolate, can e'er return.

O Attic shape! Fair attitude! with brede
  Of marble men and maidens overwrought,
With forest branches and the trodden weed;
  Thou, silent form, dost tease us out of thought
As doth eternity: Cold Pastoral!
  When old age shall this generation waste,
    Thou shalt remain, in midst of other woe
  Than ours, a friend to man, to whom thou say'st,
'Beauty is truth, truth beauty,' – that is all
    Ye know on earth, and all ye need to know.

1   *Look for a central opposition in the poem*

The instruction to look for an opposition is very straightforward, but there might well be times when you cannot see one. At such times you can call upon your knowledge of the tensions that recur in poetry, and also make use of what you have learnt of the writer so far. This should help you to understand why Keats starts by talking about the urn as expressing 'A flowery tale more sweetly than our rhyme . . . ', and then goes on to describe the picture on the sides. The urn seems to represent a world of pastoral innocence, where the brute force of the ordinary world has been eliminated. There is just a nod towards the more uncomfortable side of experience in the word 'unravish'd' in the first line: it provides a reminder that in the real world things change whereas on the vase nothing changes. We already have enough material here to move immediately to our first broader conclusion. As in 'Ode to a Nightingale', Keats sets the real world against an imagined other world, an alternative world where everything seems happy and uncomplicated.

2   *Begin to look at the details of the poem, trying to see how the poet brings the theme to life*

I want to look at how Keats develops his sense of both the negative and positive sides of his tension, and therefore have chosen the opening of the third stanza, where everything seems attractive. As I have said already in this chapter, there is no point in discussing every line of a poem; it is much more sensible to select a few lines, such as this passage, for analysis. Keats is still talking about, and to, the pictures on the urn:

> Ah happy, happy boughs! that cannot shed
>    Your leaves, nor ever bid the Spring adieu;
> And, happy melodist, unwearied,
>    For ever piping songs for ever new . . . .

The idea at the centre of these lines is still this sense of a world where nothing changes, and, as in 'Ode to a Nightingale', this harmonious vision that attracts the poet is connected with a sense of musical harmony, apparent in 'happy melodist' and 'For ever piping songs for ever new'. It is an order and harmony that reigns in both nature and music.

A different note, however, is struck by the end of this stanza. Keats goes on to talk about how far above human love is the love represented on the vase. In this ordinary world the failings of love are easy to describe, that it

> leaves a heart high-sorrowful and cloy'd,
> A burning forehead, and a parching tongue.

I am sure you will agree that these images are far less attractive than those we have looked at so far, and they are so because they relate to physical discomfort and painful extremes. A phrase such as 'parching tongue', for example, conveys economically yet forcefully the frustrations and disappointments of life as we experience it. But, as always seems to be the case in Keats's poetry, the senses are used to describe the feeling. For unpleasant ideas he uses uncomfortable sensations the body might experience, whereas for pleasant ideas he uses pictures of the senses being delighted by sound, taste, touch, smell and sight. This use of the senses seems to be central in the way that Keats brings his themes to life.

3    *Look at another section of the poem, trying to see how the poem is progressing*

We have seen the opposition in the poem – between the timeless world on the urn and this less happy world in which we live – and have seen something of how Keats presents his theme. Now, however, we need to look at how he complicates the relationship between the two sides of his opposition. I have chosen the fourth of the five stanzas of the poem to consider. The stanza begins with a series of questions:

> Who are these coming to the sacrifice?
>    To what green altar, O mysterious priest,
> Lead'st thou that heifer lowing at the skies
>    And all her silken flanks with garlands drest?

Is an attractive or unattractive picture being presented here? I can see the ways in which it could be said to be joyous, that the lines convey a sense of joyous celebration of this ancient world. Personally, however, I find these lines rather disturbing. There is something rather nasty in the idea of sacrifice, and something rather frightening about the 'mysterious priest'. While the heifer is garlanded, this does not really disguise the unpleasant fact that it is going to be killed; similarly, while the pictures on the urn are superficially happy, you only need to look a little behind the surface to see all the painfulness of reality intruding again. Having spotted the detail, we can now move out to make a broader point about the poem. Just as in 'Ode to a Nightingale', we can say, Keats shows his ability to create a more attractive alternative world which avoids the misery of this world, but it again seems to be the case that the pain of reality insinuates its way back into even the most joyful picture. It is a marvellous, wavering tension that is set up, that keeps us trembling between the dream of a better world and the reality of this world. We are for ever just about to escape from the everyday world, but for ever pulled back into this world.

### 4    Look at how the poem concludes

The urn will survive year in, year out:

> Thou shalt remain, in midst of other woe
> Than ours, a friend to man, to whom they say'st
> 'Beauty is truth, truth beauty,' – that is all
> Ye know on earth, and all ye need to know.

I have talked earlier about how a poem can have a 'twist' at the end, and this is certainly the case here, as Keats seems to provide a kind of epigrammatic solution to the issue in the poem. He appears to be saying that we can turn our backs on death and decay and turn to beauty, which is synonymous with truth. But, as attractive as these sentiments are, I am a bit reluctant to accept them. They seem a little too close to a comforting 'message', whereas the poem as a whole has suggested that the painful facts of experience cannot be ignored. There seems something a touch too glib about the way in which the vase speaks to us. I am tempted not to take these final two lines at their face value but to say that this is the rather too idyllic picture that the urn seems to convey and that truth always rather uncomfortably intrudes to disrupt such neat pictures and even such neat endings. Does not the word 'earth', after all, remind us of the grimmer truth we all share in our knowledge of death?

It might be, of course, that you totally disagree, that you feel Keats has a kind of 'answer' at the end of this poem, but that freedom of interpretation is quite all right, provided that your views grow out of the evidence of the poem itself. As I say, however, my view tends towards the feeling that Keats sets up a tension in the poem that is not fully resolved, and that much of the pleasure we derive from the poem stems from the play between the dream of a better world and the awareness of the harsh facts of this world.

5   *Sum up your sense of the poem as a whole, and your sense of the writer so far*

The way in which I have described Keats as setting up a problem but not providing an answer in his poem will be true of the works of many poets. Poets repeatedly set up a tension between how things are and how they would like things to be. Such poems appeal to our desire for order yet also acknowledge our awareness of life's disorder. The poet does not need a 'message'; it is enough that he sets up and develops his theme in an interesting way. An awareness of this pattern in poetry will help you with a great many poets, but what you are always after with an individual poet is a sense of his uniqueness, and this brief discussion of 'Ode on a Grecian Urn' should have strengthened the view I am developing of Keats. What in particular I feel I can add to my conclusions on 'Ode to a Nightingale' is a sharper awareness of how Keats's poetry sets the pains of reality against dreams of something better. It is not just that I have seen him use this theme again but that I have moved a little closer to seeing how consistently he uses sensory images to convey both joy and pain.

A look at a third poem by Keats should fill out the picture a bit more, and indeed probably provide me with quite enough material and ideas overall to tackle most examination questions on Keats. The third poem I have selected is another of his odes, **'To Autumn'**:

> Season of mists and mellow fruitfulness,
>   Close bosom-friend of the maturing sun;
> Conspiring with him how to load and bless
>   With fruit the vines that round the thatch-eves run;

To bend with apples the moss'd cottage-trees,
    And fill all fruit with ripeness to the core;
        To swell the gourd, and plump the hazel shells
    With a sweet kernel; to set budding more,
And still more, later flowers for the bees,
Until they think warm days will never cease,
        For Summer has o'er-brimm'd their clammy cells.

Who hath not seen thee oft amid thy store?
    Sometimes whoever seeks abroad may find
Thee sitting careless on a granary floor,
    Thy hair soft-lifted by the winnowing wind;
Or on a half-reap'd furrow sound asleep,
    Drows'd with the fume of poppies, while thy hook
        Spares the next swath and all its twined flowers:
And sometimes like a gleaner thou dost keep
    Steady thy laden head across a brook;
    Or by a cyder-press, with patient look,
        Thou watchest the last oozings hours by hours.

Where are the songs of Spring? Ay, where are they?
    Think not of them, thou hast thy music too, –
While barred clouds bloom the soft-dying day,
    And touch the stubble-plains with rosy hue;
        Then in a wailful choir the small gnats mourn
            Among the river sallows, borne aloft
            Or sinking as the light wind lives or dies;
And full-grown lambs loud bleat from hilly bourn;
    Hedge-crickets sing; and now with treble soft
    The red-breast whistles from a garden-croft;
        And gathering swallows twitter in the skies.

1    *Look for a central opposition in the poem*

I looked at the opening stanza for a long time, but have to admit
that no real sense of an opposition struck me. It does seem to be a
picture of pure perfection, with a beautiful and rich sense of nature
overflowing with good things. I know enough about Keats's poetry
by now, however, to guess that the implicit tension must be with
the fact that life is not always so wonderful, that decay and death
also exist. Indeed, it is just possible to find a negative note in the

line 'Until they think warm days will never cease'. This does indirectly draw attention to the fact that this wonderful season will not last for ever.

2   *Begin to look at the details of the poem, trying to see how the poet brings his theme to life*

I shall stay with this first stanza to consider the ways in which Keats creates his positive picture. As in his other poems, it is a tangible world. It is rich and abundant, but also mellow and moderate. I am particularly struck by the description of 'the vines that round the thatch-eves run . . . ': there seems a very close connection between the world of nature and the world of man, as represented by the thatched cottage. But it is not just the words that create the positive impression: there is symmetry in the construction of the lines. Look, for example, at the beautiful balance of 'Season of mists and mellow fruitfulness', where the two halves of the line seem to match each other perfectly. This sense of order in the shape of the verse helps support the idea of a perfect, well-balanced and well-ordered world. What is also apparent in this first stanza, however, is that, unlike in the other two poems we have looked at, the ideal world is not one that the poet has to imagine. It is the real season of autumn.

And it seems to dominate the poem. It is very difficult to find anything negative. The first example I can come up with is the opening of the third stanza:

Where are the songs of Spring? Ay, where are they?
Think not of them, thou hast thy music too . . . .

Just for a moment, a questioning tone intrudes into the poem, but any hint of a problem is pushed aside. The whole poem seems dominated by the positive, rich sense of autumn. The obvious point we can extrapolate from this is that the poem conveys a richer, more positive sense than the other poems we have looked at.

3   *Look at another section of the poem, trying to see how the poem is progressing*

Indeed, is there any tension in the poem, or is it just a simple, but gloriously successful, celebration of nature? Let us look at a few more lines from the last stanza:

> While barred clouds bloom the soft-dying day,
>   And touch the stubble-plains with rosy hue;
>     Then in a wailful choir the small gnats mourn . . . .

What is apparent here is that slightly more negative notes do intrude; there is talk of death in the 'soft-dying day' and the use of the word 'mourn'. Thoughts of death have therefore broken into the poem, but, unlike in the other two poems we have considered, I do not feel that the happy mood is undercut. It is as if even death has a place in the larger pattern of the seasons, and this in no way undermines the beauty of nature.

4   *Look at how the poem concludes*

The closing lines of the poem are as follows:

> The redbreast whistles from a garden-croft;
>   And gathering swallows twitter in the skies.

Here are signs of change: the redbreast signals the coming of winter, and the swallows are about to migrate. But this is all perfectly natural, all part of a larger cyclic pattern in nature.

5   *Sum up your sense of the poem as a whole, and your sense of the writer so far*

There is something very satisfying about a poem where the sense of order is allowed to dominate. It is as if the poet has got on top of the problems and disorder of life, and perceived a pattern and order in experience. And this is perhaps why 'To Autumn' is the most comforting of Keats's odes to read, but perhaps some of the other poems are more challenging in that they are less tidy and reassuring than 'To Autumn'. There is, however, absolutely no reason why you should value some of his poems more than others. The important point is to realise what is happening in the poems, the way they set up an opposition, the way in which that opposition can be kept tense and wavering, and yet how in 'To Autumn' a sense of order is allowed to dominate.

Obviously, this by no means exhausts what can be said about Keats's poetry, but I hope it is clear by now that methodical work on a series of poems will enable you to build up a view of the author. As you turn to fresh poems, try to add to what you have established. You might, for example, decide to look at one or more of Keats's narrative poems (I look at one of them in Chapter 5). On the basis of what we have established so far, it seems reasonable to assume that his narrative poems will be set in imagined, perhaps almost fairy-story-like worlds, but that the cold chill of the real world will intrude even into fairy-land. If you can get hold of the central pattern of poems in that kind of crisp, no-nonsense way, then you have laid all the necessary foundations for making a full analysis of the poem, and, eventually, a full analysis of the writer. Remember that you are never in pursuit of a complex philosophy in an author's work. All you are interested in is how he uses language to bring important, but familiar, themes to life. And, more often than not, what you will find yourself identifying at the centre of a poem is an unstable balance, as the writer plays off our desire for something positive against our cruel awareness of what is negative in life. Such poetry is rewarding because it holds out a tantalising glimpse of harmony while at the same time making us confront life as it is. Only very occasionally, as in 'To Autumn', will the sense of harmony dominate the equation. A lot of this should be apparent again as we look at the work of another writer, the twentieth-century poet Wilfred Owen.

## Wilfred Owen

The whole basis of the method of analysis I am presenting in this book starts with searching for an opposition in a poem. Wilfred Owen, at first sight, might seem to be a writer whose works cannot be built on an opposition in that his whole picture appears entirely negative and depressing. Whereas Keats might tantalise us with visions of perfection, Owen might seem to be a writer who can only appal us with visions of horror. This is because Owen was a poet of the First World War, who wrote chiefly of the horrors of war. As with many of his generation, his life was tragically short. He was killed in action in 1918, aged twenty-five, one week before the end of the war, but left a collection of brilliant and moving poems. They are poems which are easy to understand because their subject is so terrifyingly plain. They are also, however, poems which it can prove difficult to discuss because there might not seem much to say other than paraphrasing his words on the horrors of war. And an opposition might not be apparent, as the whole picture is so depressing and frightening.

Rather than continue in these general terms, however, let us start building a picture of Owen as a poet, starting with his poem **'Anthem for Doomed Youth'**. I shall employ exactly the same analytic steps as in the first half of this chapter.

What passing-bells for these who die as cattle?
   – Only the monstrous anger of the guns.
   Only the stuttering rifles' rapid rattle
Can patter out their hasty orisons.
No mockeries now for them; no prayers nor bells,
   Nor any voice of mourning save the choirs, –
The shrill, demented choirs of wailing shells;
   And bugles calling for them from sad shires.

What candles may be held to speed them all?
   Not in the hands of boys, but in their eyes
Shall shine the holy glimmers of good-byes.
   The pallor of girls' brows shall be their pall;
Their flowers the tenderness of patient minds,
And each slow dusk a drawing-down of blinds.

It is easy to see that this is a powerful poem about men killed in war, but after saying that you might be uncertain what to say next. The temptation is to lapse into summary. What you need to do, however, is search for an opposition.

## 1   *Look for a central opposition in the poem*

The main impression the poem offers is of the utter and total waste of war, of men slaughtered like cattle. Shocking as this is, however, the idea would carry little force unless there was something in the poem to set against this sense of waste. What, in fact, is set against it is the idea of some kind of anthem, or tribute, or something that marks their death. That would seem to represent some gesture against the meaningless waste of it all. It would at least represent a civilised mark of respect for the dead. Can you see, therefore, how there is an opposition at the heart of the poem, an opposition which searches for something better to redeem in some way the brutal reality of war?

2  *Begin to look at the details of the poem, trying to see how the poet
   brings his theme to life*

Some of the details will create an impression of the horror of war,
whereas other details will try to create a sense of something more
positive. Both aspects are apparent in the opening line, where
'passing-bells' is set against 'those who die as cattle'. Both phrases
are emotive: 'passing-bells' seems civilised, the traditional way of
commemorating loss, but the polite phrase is set against the
starkness of 'cattle'. It could be called a civilised-*versus*-uncivilised
tension in the stanza, and the tension is expressed in opposed lines
of imagery. On the one hand is the idea of a 'voice of mourning',
but it is as if the civilised voice has given way to 'monstrous anger'
and 'stuttering rifles'. Everything has been reduced to an animal
status, where even speech is lost. And, when Owen speaks of 'hasty
orisons', we notice the disparity between the elevated word 'orisons'
and the brutal reality of war. At points such as this the idea of a
religious tribute seems almost a mockery, as if the situation is so
unprecedented and extreme that the old forms can no longer cope
with it. As always, however, I do want to make the point that the
stanza could be interpreted differently. There is no inherently
correct meaning. Every reader will see the matter slightly differently.
In a way, my reading is neither here nor there, for what I am really
anxious to get across here is how criticism should build a view from
the text in the kind of way I have tried to illustrate.

3  *Look at another section of the poem, trying to see how the poem is
   progressing*

In the second stanza Owen continues the idea of some kind of
tribute or mark of respect for the dead. There is a series of funeral
images, with 'candles', 'holy glimmers', the 'pall' and 'flowers'. The
relevance of the funeral service is that it treats death with dignity,
but what strikes me in this stanza is that the real force that is set
against death is the feelings of those left behind. Indeed, the second
verse stresses how tribute will essentially come from the eyes, faces
and minds of those left behind, and that is a more adequate
'anthem' for those that are gone; there is the shocking fact of death,
but also the concern of their loved ones.

4   *Look at how the poem concludes*

The final line is 'And each slow dusk a drawing-down of blinds'. It is a quiet and touching picture, far removed from the brutality of the opening of the poem. Yet here, I think, we come on to the essentially traditional nature of Owen's poem, for what Owen sets against death is love, that love is the only meaningful thing in a cruel world.

5   *Sum up your sense of the poem as a whole, and your sense of the writer so far*

Having looked closely at a poem it is essential to pull back and attempt to sum up what you have established. The points I feel I can now make about Owen are as follows: that initially what makes such an impression is the forceful picture he presents of a terrible situation. On reflection, however, I can see that there is a mixture of old and new in this poem. It is, as so many poems are, a poem about love in a world where death exists, but what makes it so new is that Owen has found a language adequate to expressing the horror of war. But horrifying images on their own would not be enough: he has to set an idea of love against his vision of waste.

I have drawn far less attention to my method of analysis as I have gone on in this chapter, but I hope it is still clear what steps you can take with a poem, and essentially how straightforward your approach can be. By starting with the idea of a broad opposition, and then looking closely at the poem, taking care to pull back and sum up along the way, you will find yourself managing to put together your own distinctive and well-substantiated reading of any poem. But one poem only begins to establish a case about a writer. In order to add to our view of Owen, let me now turn to his poem **'Strange Meeting'**:

It seemed that out of battle I escaped
Down some profound dull tunnel, long since scooped
Through granites which titanic wars had groined.

Yet also there encumbered sleepers groaned,
Too fast in thought or death to be bestirred.

Then, as I probed them, one sprang up, and stared
With piteous recognition in fixed eyes,
Lifting distressful hands as if to bless.
And by his smile, I knew that sullen hall, –
By his dead smile I knew we stood in Hell.

With a thousand pains that vision's face was grained;
Yet no blood reached there from the upper ground,
And no guns thumped, or down the flues made moan.
'Strange friend,' I said, 'here is no cause to mourn.'
'None,' said that other, 'save the undone years,
The hopelessness. Whatever hope is yours,
Was my life also; I went hunting wild
After the wildest beauty in the world,
Which lies not calm in eyes, or braided hair,
But mocks the steady running of the hour,
And if it grieves, grieves richlier than here.
For by my glee might many men have laughed,
And of my weeping something had been left,
Which must die now. I mean the truth untold,
The pity of war, the pity war distilled.
Now men will go content with what we spoiled,
Or, discontent, boil bloody, and be spilled.
They will be swift with swiftness of the tigress.
None will break ranks, though nations trek from progress.
Courage was mine, and I had mystery,
Wisdom was mine, and I had mastery;
To miss the march of this retreating world
Into vain citadels that are not walled.
Then, when much blood had clogged their chariot-wheels,
I would go up and wash them from sweet wells,
Even with truths that lie too deep for taint.
I would have poured my spirit without stint
But not through wounds; not on the cess of war.
Foreheads of men had bled where no wounds were.

I am the enemy you killed, my friend.
I knew you in this dark: for so you frowned
Yesterday through me as you jabbed and killed.
I parried; but my hands were loath and cold.
Let us sleep now . . . .

1    *Look for a central opposition in the poem*

This is a longer poem than 'Anthem for Doomed Youth', so the
most practical approach is to search for a significant opposition in
the opening lines:

> It seemed that out of battle I escaped
> Down some profound dull tunnel, long since scooped
> Through granites which titanic wars had groined.

The word that catches my eye is 'escaped' in the first line. It
immediately confronts us with the idea that there must be some
alternative to the horror of war. But, while that expectation is set
up, the poem frustrates it, for the 'escape' is just as terrifying as
war as Owen presents us with a nightmare vision of being caught
in a terrible, dark tunnel. There is thus nothing really positive at
the opening of the poem, but can you see how Owen is touching on
our need to find an escape from life's most terrible experiences?

2    *Begin to look at the details of the poem, trying to see how the poet
     brings his theme to life*

What happens as the poem develops is that the narrator comes face
to face with a dead man. A dead voice speaks:

> Whatever hope is yours,
> Was my life also; I went hunting wild
> After the wildest beauty in the world . . . .

This is again an escape from the present reality, on this occasion an
escape into the recent past when hopes existed, and the wildest
pursuit of a young man was for a young woman. That world has
been smashed, however, and most of the poem confronts us with
the horrors of the present:

> Now men will go content with what we spoiled,
> Or, discontent, boil bloody, and be spilled.
> They will be swift with swiftness of the tigress.
> None will break ranks, though nations trek from progress.

These sentences are complex and difficult to understand, but set about interpreting them in a methodical way. Start by asking yourself whether an attractive or an unattractive impression is conveyed. My answer would be that the very fact that the sentences are difficult to follow suggests something unattractive. And it is unattractive because the vision presented is of a world where values and standards have gone, where men veer between extremes. They either passively accept everything or become violent. The idea that comes across to me from this is that what is destroyed is a sense of humanity. This is evident in the use of animal imagery: it is as if men will behave either like fierce animals or like docile robots.

3   *Look at another section of the poem, trying to see how the poem is progressing*

The central opposition in the poem is an idea of war versus escape from war. This is mainly presented as an escape into the past when civilised behaviour existed. War not only destroys men but also destroys all mankind's civilised values. I shall now move to a passage from later in the poem to see whether and how this idea is developed. It is a section where the dead voice continues to speak of the past:

> Courage was mine, and I had mystery,
> Wisdom was mine, and I had mastery:
> To miss the march of this retreating world
> Into vain citadels that are not walled.
> Then, when much blood had clogged their chariot-wheels,
> I would go up and wash them from sweet wells . . . .

Again the lines are hard to understand. If you find it difficult to follow them it is because Owen is expressing his ideas in involved and complex sentences, so let us start by trying to decide why. The best answer I can come up with is that he is talking about the complex destruction of a whole array of civilised values, and his sentences therefore have to become complicated to convey the complex nature of his theme. This becomes more apparent if we contrast the complicated sentence about 'vain citadels that are not walled' with the first two lines of this extract. There seems something positive and easy to grasp about concepts such as 'courage' and 'wisdom', which existed in the past, and this sense of positive human qualities is reinforced by the pattern of the lines.

They are symmetrical and balanced, four perfectly balanced phrases, and the correspondence of sound between 'mystery' and 'mastery' adds to that sense of neatness. But that civilised, simple order of the past has yielded to a tortuous present.

When I look at the phrase 'vain citadels that are not walled', two ideas occur to me. One is that 'vain citadels' sounds inflated, as if this world has abandoned order and moderation and wisdom and gone off in vain pursuits. The other point is that 'not walled' suggests a lack of boundaries and defining lines, as if the old containing order has broken down and disappeared. And this world that has come into existence is bloody and cruel, with only the voice of the dead man seeming to speak up for decent behaviour, as it speaks about washing away the blood.

### 4   Look at how the poem concludes

How can Owen end a poem such as this? 'Anthem for Doomed Youth' ended positively with the idea of love, but in this poem civilised values seem a thing of the past. So, how can the poem end? The only way to find out is to look closely at the closing lines. The voice again speaks to the poet:

> I am the enemy you killed, my friend.
> I knew you in this dark: for so you frowned
> Yesterday through me as you jabbed and killed.
> I parried; but my hands were loath and cold.
> Let us sleep now . . . .

All that might strike you here at first is the brutality, conveyed well in the ideas and in the use of a harsh phrase such as 'jabbed and killed', but what I find most interesting are the words 'the enemy you killed, my friend'. Even amidst death there is a voice than can understand concepts such as friendship.

### 5   Sum up your sense of the poem as a whole, and your sense of the writer so far

Throughout 'Strange Meeting' we find a concept of civilised, humane behaviour that is set against the present reality of killing and used to judge it. That is my conclusion on this poem, but I also want to add to my overall sense of Owen as a poet. What I think 'Strange Meeting' adds to my earlier impressions is a stronger awareness of how Owen is a poet who sets civilised values against the destruction of war. In 'Anthem for Doomed Youth' the central positive value was love. If we consider the words of the dead voice in 'Strange Meeting', I think we could say that the positive force here could also be described as love, but another way of putting it would be to talk about a whole concept of a humane man that existed before the world degenerated into extremes, extremes of total lack of feeling and extreme anger.

These impressions of Owen should develop again with a look at a third poem by him. This is **'Dulce et Decorum Est'**: the title is taken from the Latin saying 'Dulce et decorum est pro patria mori', meaning 'It is sweet and fitting to lay down one's life for one's country.'

Bent double, like old beggars under sacks,
Knock-kneed, coughing like hags, we cursed through sludge,
Till on the haunting flares we turned our backs
And towards our distant rest began to trudge.
Men marched asleep. Many had lost their boots
But limped on, blood-shod. All went lame; all blind;
Drunk with fatigue; deaf even to the hoots
Of tired, outstripped Five-Nines that dropped behind.

Gas! Gas! Quick boys! – An ecstasy of fumbling,
Fitting the clumsy helmets just in time;
But someone still was yelling out and stumbling
And flound'ring like a man in fire or lime . . .
Dim, through the misty panes and thick green light,
As under a green sea, I saw him drowning.

In all my dreams, before my helpless sight,
He plunges at me, guttering, choking, drowning.

If in some smothering dreams you too could pace
Behind the wagon that we flung him in,
And watch the white eyes writhing in his face,
His hanging face, like a devil's sick of sin;
If you could hear, at every jolt, the blood

Come gargling from the froth-corrupted lungs,
Obscene as cancer, bitter as the cud
Of vile, incurable sores on innocent tongues, –
My friend, you would not tell with such high zest
To children ardent for some desperate glory,
The old Lie: Dulce et decorum est
Pro patria mori.

1   *Look for a central opposition in the poem*

As this chapter has developed I have tended to let the method of
analysis speak for itself, but it might be a good idea if I again
provide a few pointers as I look at this last poem in this chapter.
The first move is, of course, to look for a central opposition, an
opposition which might be implicit rather than explicit. Here, for
example, there is a terrible picture of human suffering with no real
alternative presented, but a civilised alternative is, to my mind,
implicit. The form this takes is essentially that people be allowed to
be human. War is presented as dehumanising.

2   *Begin to look at the details of the poem, trying to see how the poet
    brings his theme to life*

With any poem, once you have established an opposition, you need
to look at how the details of the poem flesh out that idea. What
interests me here is the way the soldiers are described as being 'like
old beggars' and 'like hags'. They have been reduced to something
less than men, an idea which is sustained in the images of physical
shortcomings: they are, variously, lame, blind, drunk and deaf.
Can you see how simple the essential method of the poem is? A
basic idea of human dignity and people being robbed of their
dignity, but Owen finding the words to bring that idea disturbingly
to life. Many of the images are so direct yet brilliantly effective. If
we consider the simple phrase 'Many had lost their boots', there
seems nothing to it at all, but think about how it presents an image
of men robbed of their dignity and the protection that civilisation
takes for granted.
  The second stanza is equally powerful:

Gas! Gas! Quick boys! – An ecstasy of fumbling,
Fitting the clumsy helmets just in time;

> But someone still was yelling out and stumbling
> And flound'ring like a man in fire or lime . . .
> Dim, through the misty panes and thick green light,
> As under a green sea, I saw him drowning.

It is again the case that Owen finds words that convey an impression of men robbed of their dignity: they are 'yelling', 'stumbling' and 'flound'ring'. But what also comes across to me in these lines is that the situation is so extreme that it becomes a kind of bizarre nightmare. This is especially apparent as he looks at the man dying, staring through the fog of his gas-mask: he is, paradoxically, both distanced from the situation and yet deeply affected by it. The scene is so effective because it conveys such a powerful sense of the frailty and vulnerability of the human body.

3   *Look at another section of the poem, trying to see how the poem is progressing*

A look at a later extract from the poem should reveal how Owen develops this idea:

> If in some smothering dreams you too could pace
> Behind the wagon that we flung him in,
> And watch the white eyes writhing in his face,
> His hanging face, like a devil's sick of sin . . .

At the centre of this extract is the idea of indignities piled upon the human body. This idea comes across graphically in the picture of the body being flung on the wagon, and then in the image of the face writhing in pain. What is the alternative to this? That, in a way, is there in the words 'you too could pace / Behind the wagon . . . '. All that is being asked for is a chance for men to walk upright in dignity and with self-respect.

4   *Look at how the poem concludes*

The poem, having presented these grisly pictures, says that anyone who had seen such things would not:

> tell with such high zest
> To children ardent for some desperate glory,
> The old Lie: Dulce et decorum est
> Pro patria mori.

Why are these concluding lines so effective? The obvious answer is that there is something shocking in saying such things to children, but I think more is involved than that. The way I should put it is that the use of Latin makes the idea sound dignified, but what the poem has shown is men robbed of every scrap of dignity. There is a cruel disparity between the reality of war and this inflated Latin discourse; it is like hiding inside a dead language to avoid facing the truth.

5   *Sum up your sense of the poem as a whole, and your sense of the writer so far*

At the end of a poem we need to stand back and sum up. What, if anything, though, can I add to what I have said already? Well, to a large extent I have simply confirmed my earlier impression that Owen's poems work on a contrast between civilised and uncivilised behaviour. But I think I do have a fuller understanding now of how the poems constantly invoke, despite all the horrors of so much of the description, an idea of humane and ordered conduct. It is an idea which is perhaps inherent in the very existence of the poems themselves. Nothing could be more shapeless and chaotic than war, yet Owen confronts war through poetry, and in that we have the idea of an order coming up against total disorder. It is again apparent in his frequently used images of sound, of men reduced to groaning or yelling. His own poems, however, embody the power of speech to confront the world, even a world where ugly sounds might seem to have taken over from speech.

What this brings me back to is the way in which the same pattern seems to underlie so much poetry. There are tremendous differences of subject and theme between poems, but there is a very real sense in which poets turn again and again to search for something positive, something orderly in a disorderly world. If you come to an individual poet with that kind of sense of the patterns that underlie poetry in general, you will find yourself making rapid progress with the poet in question – provided, that is, that you focus closely on individual poems, so that you can get close to a sense of how any poet is unique.

It is this method, of how to combine broad ideas and close attention to the text, that I have tried to illustrate in this chapter. I have dealt with two particular poets, but I do hope it is plain that the kind of method I have used can work with any writer. And really, if you follow this method and keep on niggling away at writers, there is no limit to what you can establish within your coherent framework of analysis. I have cut off the discussions rather than let them become too involved, but if you try the approach recommended here you should find yourself developing your own confident view of a writer, and a view which might, as you probe away at poems, become very complex indeed. It might also enable you to come up with very different views of Keats or Owen from those I have developed here, as it is intended to be a method that will enable you to put together your own distinctive view of a writer.

The method depends totally, of course, upon actually working on the text. A question this might prompt is whether there is any need to find out about the author's life and times, or to read any critical books, or to approach the writer in any other way. My answer to this is that there might well come a point when you want to discover more, when you feel the need to put the poems in context, or discover what other people think of them, but such things come later. What it all has to start with, and what should absorb you most of the time, is reading and working on the poems themselves. As you do this, what might well happen is that you find yourself becoming more and more interested in the mechanics of poetry, what techniques the writer can call upon to make his work effective, and it is to this, the techniques and devices of poetry, that I turn more fully in the next chapter.

# 3

# The language and structure of poetry

A POEM makes its impact because of the special way in which the poet says what he has to say. It follows from this that we cannot just talk about the meaning of a poem, but that we must also look at its language and structure. Indeed, we are unlikely to grasp fully the content of a poem without considering its form. Unfortunately, as examiners know all too well from the experience of reading hundreds of examination answers, technical analysis of poetry often amounts to little more than a rather pointless listing of the devices the poet uses, such as rhyme, alliteration and assonance. Study of form need not, however, be approached in such an arid way. What you have to get clear is that form is far more than the clothes in which the poet dresses his ideas. Indeed, the meaning of a poem is only created by every detailed choice the writer makes about how to write the poem. If this sounds rather vague, I hope things will become clearer in the course of this chapter as I describe ways of talking about how poets use language and structure to create meaning. Much of what I say will, in fact, cover ground already covered in my first two chapters, where I have already focused heavily on form, but I shall try to explain some aspects of form more fully here.

This is not, however, a highly technical chapter. There is a specialised vocabulary which can be employed to describe specific effects in poems, and at some stage you are likely to come across terms such as 'iambic pentameter' and 'trochee', but it is possible to discuss poetry without knowing these words. Indeed, it can sometimes be an advantage not to know them, as what you should be concerned to do as a critic is to describe, rather than merely name, the effect you have spotted in a poem. My emphasis the whole time, therefore, is going to be on how to talk about language and structure in a very direct way, seeing how the choices the poet has made help create the meaning of a poem. It is for this reason that I have decided to omit information about such subjects as metre and how to scan lines. It could be argued that such topics should be included in a book about how to study a poet, but I want to go directly for the way in which the words a poet uses, and the way the poet combines and patterns them, create meaning. Rather than talk any more in general terms, however, let me turn to a specific poet.

## Thomas Hardy

Thomas Hardy is best known as a novelist, writing works such as *Far from the Madding Crowd* and *Tess of the d'Urbervilles*, but he also produced hundreds of short poems. What I intend to do here is look at three of these in order to gain a sense of what Hardy was like as a poet. As this is a chapter about form, I shall obviously discuss the method of these poems quite extensively, but let me make it clear that my general approach is the same as in my first two chapters. Indeed, I shall employ exactly the same steps as I have done already, the only difference being that I shall pay slightly more attention to the form of each poem at each stage of the discussion. The poem I start with, **'The Voice'**, is one that seems to be included whenever a selection of Hardy's poems is published. I can, therefore, be confident that it is a poem worth studying, and it is also a fair bet that it will tell me quite a lot about Hardy as a poet.

Woman much missed, how you call to me, call to me,
Saying that now you are not as you were
When you had changed from the one who was all to me,
But as at first, when our day was fair.

Can it be you that I hear? Let be view you, then,
Standing as when I drew near to the town
Where you would wait for me: yes, as I knew you then,
Even to the original air-blue gown!

Or is it only the breeze, in its listlessness
Travelling across the wet mead to me here,
You being ever dissolved to wan wistlessness,
Heard no more again far or near?

> Thus I; faltering forward,
> Leaves around me falling,
> Wind oozing thin through the thorn from norward,
> And the woman calling.

## 1 Look for a central opposition in the poem

With a short poem, it is possible to search for an opposition in the poem as a whole. What strikes me here is that there is an opposition between the past, which was a time of happiness, and the present, which is a time of unhappiness. Happiness was associated with a woman, who is no longer present. Hardy does not actually say that she is dead, but perhaps most readers would assume that she is. This could be because we search for a familiar pattern in poems and know that poets often set love against death. It is certainly clear here that the memories that stir Hardy's heart are memories of love. The poem is, then, working with a familiar theme, and if it does make an impact it must be because of Hardy's skill as a poet in presenting a familiar topic in a new way. We therefore need to look closely at how he writes in order to capture the essence of the poem.

## 2 Begin to look at the details of the poem, trying to see how the poet brings his theme to life

In the first line, 'Woman, much missed, how you call to me, call to me', a very strong sense is established of just how much Hardy misses the woman. The moment we start trying to explain how the line creates this effect, we have embarked upon a discussion of Hardy's technique. We have moved beyond a sense of language as merely conveying information, and have begun to look at how language can create a mood or tone and suggest far more than is being directly said. This might sound complex, but the techniques employed are straightforward. Look here, for example, at the words 'much missed'. The meaning of the words tells us that he misses her, but the fact that the two words begin with the same letter – that is to say, that Hardy uses alliteration – pulls the two words together and emphasises the meaning. This is how alliteration works; words beginning with the same letter are not chosen because of any special meaning in the letters themselves but rather because the alliteration serves to link and emphasise the words. The idea of missing the woman is then further reinforced in the repetition of 'call to me', so that it seems like an echo, possibly an echo from the past. It is already the case in the poem, then, that more is being suggested than is directly stated. The simple techniques employed add nuances of meaning to the poem. Most of the time in analysing the form of poetry, this is what you will be pointing to: how the choice and combination of words convey meanings. You are not searching for 'hidden' meanings, simply examining how the writing creates a certain complexity of mood or feeling.

It is not just the choice and combination of words that matter, however, but also the larger pattern of a few lines or a stanza. In this poem, for example, the second stanza is one of happy recall, whereas the first stanza is largely concerned with confused feelings. The words of the stanzas tell us this, but we can also point to another way in which a sense of security is created in one stanza and a sense of insecurity in the other. Consider these lines:

> Standing as when I drew near to the town
> Where you would wait for me: yes, as I knew you then,
> Even to the original air-blue gown!

These are confident statements, ordered, balanced and complete. It is generally the case that a reassuring feel is established if the two halves of a line balance, and this is certainly the case in 'Where you would wait for me: yes, as I knew you then'. Such symmetry in the structure of the line reinforces, and at the same time deepens, its meaning: a sense of well-being and security is conveyed through the construction of the line. In this stanza as a whole, there is balance and order in the structure of the verse which adds to the overall meaning of the poem.

As against this, the first stanza gets tied up in knots:

> Saying that now you are not as you were
> When you had changed from the one who was all to me . . . .

This is an involved sentence which, as it goes on, seems to tie itself up in a tangle. Why does Hardy write like this? The simple fact is that structuring the sentence in this manner suggests a mind in a state of turmoil and confusion. And what is true in this poem should prove to be the case in most poems. If, therefore, we look at both the words and combination of words, and how the lines of a poem are put together, we should gain a fuller sense of the nuances and subtleties of meaning of a poem. This is not to say that there is a single correct meaning that can be arrived at. We are looking at the way in which language and structure create meaning, but, as we are looking at what is being suggested rather than directly stated, each of us will arrive at our own sense of the meaning conveyed.

The techniques that are central in creating meaning are, however, few in number and fairly straightforward, although capable of producing an endless variety of meanings. In the case of structure, it is always worth looking for ordered lines and more tangled lines. Ordered, symmetrical lines will generally suggest a positive mood or positive sentiment; knotted and confused lines will generally suggest knotted and confused feelings. Knowing this can help a lot when you have to study a difficult poem. There are some poems where the syntax becomes so involved that the sense of the lines becomes almost impossible to follow, but an easy way of coping with such passages is to tell yourself that at these points the poet must be attempting to convey a sense of intellectual or emotional confusion. And what you can also tell yourself is that at some point in the same poem the writer is likely to offer a far less tangled vision of how he would like life to be or what he sees as a simple ideal.

These kinds of patterns in verse structure are found in the works of all poets. In a very similar way, certain patterns of opposition recur in the words of poetry, always carrying much the same implications. The most common such effect we can point to is the one of light and dark imagery. In 'The Voice', Hardy recalls a time when 'our day was fair', but the present seems a blind stagger in the winter darkness. In all poetry, light is positive and dark negative in this kind of way, and there is barely a poem in existence that does not call upon this opposition in some shape or form. There are, however, other and equally effective ways of creating a positive or negative impression. Poets can, for example, exploit the fact that we find the solid and tangible reassuring, whereas the fluid and abstract can prove unnerving. In Keats's 'Ode to a Nightingale', part of the attraction of the world of the nightingale is its solidity as opposed to a world where men are wasting away, and in Hardy's poem the woman, as presented in the second stanza, is solid and tangible, whereas in the next verse everything dissolves. A reassuring sense can also be established in poetry by a specific sense of place. In the second stanza of 'The Voice', there is the precision of the phrase 'near to the town', whereas in the rest of the poem it is apparent that the narrator is wandering and lost. This is again an opposition all poets employ: the security of a specific place as against being lost in an anonymous and threatening world.

What is also generally true is that, if a writer uses certain words or ideas to create one side of an opposition, then he or she is bound to use the appropriate words that suggest the other side of the opposition. In 'The Voice', for example, we find the past described as fair and sunny, so it comes as no surprise that the present, as conveyed in the third stanza, is wet. In the same way, Hardy's movements in the past were purposeful as he 'drew near to the town', but now he is only 'faltering forward'. Such oppositions in the poem not only help define the subject matter of the work but also add to its meaning, so that we get a complex sense of the happiness he once knew and the unhappiness that he is experiencing now. As so much more is being implied than is ever directly stated, our best chance of arriving at a full sense of the meaning of the poem is to focus on its technique, so that we can pursue the nuances of implied meaning.

3   *Look at another section of the poem, trying to see how the poem is progressing*

I hope it is apparent that the approach I am describing is straightforward and methodical. What unnerves many people when they have to write about technique is the feeling that there must be something obscure in the method of a complex and impressive poem, something mysterious you are being asked to explain. Perhaps it is impossible to get at the ultimate secret of the technique of great poets, but, as I have indicated, we can grasp the methods all poets turn to again and again to help make their themes come to life. We can see this again in the third stanza of 'The Voice':

> Or is it only the breeze, in its listlessness
> Travelling across the wet mead to me here,
> You being ever dissolved to wan wistlessness,
> Heard no more again far or near?

The confident crispness of the second stanza has disappeared. The rhythm is noticeably different. But, having said that, how do we describe the rhythm? There is, in fact, a very simple method for finding the words to describe the rhythm of a passage; the answer is to look at the words of the lines which will provide you with the descriptive words you need. The appropriate word here is 'listlessness': there is something listless, exhausted and depressing about the whole movement of this stanza.

What is being said in the stanza is, of course, also depressing. You would need to examine the words to see what precise mood is being established, always remembering, of course, that this is also partly defined by the difference between the words used here and opposing words elsewhere in the poem. The solidity of the previous stanza, for example, has given way to thinness and insubstantiality here. What you are trying to define is your sense of the meaning conveyed. Hardy is not just saying that he is unhappy. Nor is he spelling out his feelings. Instead, through the use of the techniques we have looked at so far, he is suggesting a great deal. Much of the analysis of poetry must always be concerned with how the writer concentrates so much meaning into so small a space.

All the things I have discussed so far contribute to this, but the most important quality is the poet's use of imagery. Imagery covers every concrete object, action and feeling in a poem and also the use of metaphors and similes. 'The Voice', for example, starts with the image of the woman and the image of her calling: the poet is not talking in abstract terms about life but describing a particular experience in a specific context. This is a straightforward use of imagery, but the term also covers the figurative use of language in poetry: 'figurative' language is language used in a non-literal way – for example, when the poet uses a simile or metaphor. There is a very simple example in the first stanza of this poem in the phrase 'when our day was fair': a word that describes the weather is used to describe the relationship between Hardy and the woman. It is a simple way of making the idea vivid. This weather-imagery is developed in the third stanza. Hardy is obviously doing more than just describing the day; he is using words from one area of life in order to talk about another aspect of life, in this instance his feelings. The meaning is rich but imprecise, because little is being said directly but a lot is being suggested. Here, for example, the reader makes the connections between the way the breeze is blowing and Hardy's sense of emptiness and loss. There is no precise meaning stated, but we can see how the imagery is working to create a complex impression. It is this kind of use of imagery which more than anything else creates depth of meaning in a poem.

There are three ways in which I would suggest imagery contributes something to a poem. The easiest way of talking about the figurative images is simply to say that they help bring the theme of the poem vividly and memorably to life. Beyond this we can, as I have described above, talk about how imagery adds to the meaning of a poem by managing to suggest a great deal in a few words. The third way in which imagery is important is, however, slightly more complex. Imagery broadens the scope of the poem. On the surface this is just a little poem about a man feeling unhappy, but if it seems more significant it is because connections are established between the individual experience and the larger movements of nature. When Hardy employs nature images he starts to establish links between the events at the heart of the poem and larger patterns of harmony and lack of harmony that can be observed in life. By the end of the poem Hardy seems to have done more than just comment on his own feelings of loss. He seems to have made a wider statement about happiness and unhappiness as it exists in the whole order of life. And it is the use of nature-imagery that has achieved this, for he has linked one small experience with other areas of experience. Imagery in poetry repeatedly functions in this kind of way: it broadens the issue, bringing into the poem a complex sense of a wider lack of order in experience.

### 4   *Look at how the poem concludes*

We can see imagery functioning very effectively at the end of the poem:

> Thus I; faltering forward,
> Leaves around me falling,
> Wind oozing thin through the thorn from norward,
> And the woman calling.

The poem started by contrasting a happy past and the unhappy present. Here we are very much in the present, and the mood is gloomy. Yet the words of the stanza never relate this as a fact. Everything about Hardy's state of mind is suggested through imagery, the imagery of his 'faltering', the leaves falling, the cold wind and the woman calling. The images create a sense of his feelings, but a sense that will differ from reader to reader as each of us will see different implications in the images employed. But the images do not just serve to define Hardy's feelings: their presence broadens the meaning of the poem, so that we can see that Hardy is talking about death, decay and cruelty in life as a whole, about happiness and unhappiness in life.

5  *Sum up your sense of the poem as a whole, and your sense of the writer so far*

The other thing we could comment on in this last stanza of the poem is the structure of the lines, the way in which the lines do seem to falter, as if Hardy is stumbling along unhappily in a cruel and hostile world. Technical analysis of a poem amounts to nothing more than being aware of this kind of effect in the structure of the verse and of the kind of effects in the poem's use of imagery that I have described above. The actual techniques the poet employs are straightforward and common to all poets, but such simple techniqes can work to create the most complex meanings within the frame of a very small poem. Your analysis of the technique of a poem will, however, only have any point if you constantly assess how the technical feature you are looking at does add to the meaning of the poem. And this is also true at the end of the whole process, where you need to step back and sum up what you can now say about this poet that you could not have said before examining the poem. In the case of Hardy, I now feel that I can say quite a bit about him as a poet. At first sight, he struck me as a fairly accessible, fairly easy writer. I could see that he dealt with familiar themes, but an examination of 'The Voice' has shown me how interesting a writer he is. He seems to take the standard themes of love and death, and on a small scale, but, with very assured use of imagery and verse form, make us consider afresh the ghastliness of loss and the value of love in what is often a cruel world.

I now turn to another of Hardy's poems, **'The Darkling Thrush'**, to see what, if anything, I can add to this view of him as a writer.

I leant upon a coppice gate
    When Frost was spectre-gray,
And Winter's dregs made desolate
    The weakening eye of day.
The tangled bine-stems scored the sky
    Like strings of broken lyres,
And all mankind that haunted nigh
    Had sought their household fires.

The land's sharp features seemed to be
    The Century's corpse outleant,
His crypt the cloudy canopy,
    The wind his death-lament.
The ancient pulse of germ and birth
    Was shrunken hard and dry,
And every spirit upon earth
    Seemed fervourless as I.

At once a voice arose among
    The bleak twigs overhead
In a full-hearted evensong
    Of joy illimited;
An aged thrush, frail, gaunt, and small,
    In blast-beruffled plume,
Had chosen thus to fling his soul
    Upon the growing gloom.

So little cause for carolings
    Of such ecstatic sound
Was written on terrestrial things
    Afar or nigh around,
That I could think there trembled through
    His happy good-night air
Some blessed Hope, whereof he knew
    And I was unaware.

1   *Look for a central opposition in the poem*

This is a longer poem than 'The Voice', so it might be a good idea
to focus on the opening stanza in the search for an opposition:

I leant upon a coppice gate
    When Frost was spectre-gray,
And Winter's dregs made desolate
    The weakening eye of day.
The tangled bine-stems scored the sky
    Like strings of broken lyres,
And all mankind that haunted nigh
    Had sought their household fires.

When, as in this instance, an opposition is more implicit than explicit in a poem, it is necessary to call upon our awareness of the common concerns of poetry, our sense of how poetry seeks signs of order in a confusing world. We need to search for something positive within the generally depressing picture of this opening stanza. The only thing which comes into this category is the household fires image appearing in the last line after the long description of winter, yet this is enough to provide us with a sense of an opposition and a theme. There is a sense of people seeking warmth in a bleak landscape.

We could talk about how vivid Hardy's picture of winter is, but it makes more sense to start talking immediately about Hardy's imagery, for the lines depend totally upon imagery. At no stage is a theme stated. At no point are we given any direct sense of what the poem is about. Yet we know that it is more than just a piece of description; we know that some broader significance is implicit. We know this because of our instinctive grasp of how a poet employs imagery to talk about life. The only thing we have to be careful about is discovering foolish, cryptic messages in the verse, but we should not make this mistake as we know the verse must be dealing with the perennial problems that poets are always concerned with. In broad terms, winter must suggest fairly negative ideas, but we can add to this impression if we consider the particular images included which start to suggest a whole complex web of dark and wintry feelings. In 'spectre-gray' there is a sense of ghosts that make the day rather frightening; in 'Winter's dregs' Hardy suggests something exhausted and discarded; and in 'Tangled bine-stems scored the sky', there is a notion of disorder, of things being scratched and tangled. All the individual images, therefore, contribute to the picture, and what must be apparent is that far more is being suggested about winter than could ever be conveyed by an art of direct statement.

The images also serve to extend, as well as deepen, the meaning.

This is perhaps most apparent when Hardy uses the musical image 'Like strings of broken lyres'. Music suggests harmony, but this broken-lyre image suggests disharmony and discord. The inclusion of the image therefore serves to broaden the significance of the poem so that it becomes apparent that Hardy is writing about the general notions of disorder and harmony in existence. But none of this is ever stated, of course; everything is implied through the imagery.

2    *Begin to look at the details of the poem, trying to see how the poet brings his theme to life*

The way in which the imagery functions is again apparent at the beginning of the second stanza:

> The land's sharp features seemed to be
>     The Century's corpse outleant . . . .

This is a big idea, how the sight of the land suggests the sense of the body of the whole century lying dead. Can you see, however, how the image broadens the meaning again, for now the whole subject of death is brought into the poem? It adds to the poem's sense of a negative and wasted world. Yet, although the image might seem merely negative, adding to the gloomy impression in the poem, the very fact of Hardy's making the metaphorical connection between the landscape and a corpse suggests the desire of all poets to make connections and to struggle to make sense of a perplexing world. The image thus pulls in two opposed directions: it adds to the poem's sense of a panorama of disorder, yet suggests the poet's determination to try to make sense of such chaos.

3    *Look at another section of the poem, trying to see how the poem is progressing*

The structure of the two Hardy poems we have been considering is remarkably similar. A theme is set up in the first stanza, elaborated in the second, complicated in the third, and in some way resolved in the last stanza. What happens in 'The Darkling Thrush' is that Hardy introduces a positive force to set against the prevalent mood of gloom that he has established. It is the thrush that is the positive force; he hears it

> In full-hearted evensong
>> Of joy illimited . . . .

This tells us that the bird is happy, but the inclusion of the word 'evensong' adds an additional level of meaning to the poem. It is a religious term, and so there seems something spiritual about the bird, an idea which is sustained when, later in the same stanza, Hardy writes about the bird flinging 'his soul' upon the gloom. It is only an old thrush singing, but Hardy's use of imagery invests the whole story with far more significance. The basic theme is simple – here is a sign of hope in winter – but the use of imagery enriches and broadens the meaning.

4   *Look at how the poem concludes*

Let us consider the final stanza:

> So little cause for carolings
>> Of such ecstatic sound
> Was written on terrestrial things
>> Afar or nigh around,
> That I could think there trembled through
>> His happy good-night air
> Some blessed Hope, whereof he knew
>> And I was unaware.

In these lines Hardy does make a direct statement when he tells us that he imagines the bird as knowing of some 'Hope', but can you see how our examination of the use of imagery in the poem enables us to say that there is much more significance to the bird and its song than can be summed up in the one word 'Hope'? It is 'blessed Hope', and the bird's song is 'carolings': again a religious dimension is introduced; perhaps some parallel is being drawn with the birth of Christ in the bleakness of winter. The poem, as such, is suggesting far more than it actually states. Neither your account of the poem nor mine will capture any 'correct' or 'final' meaning, but we must try to grasp how the language of the poem is working to create a complex kind of meaning.

5   *Sum up your sense of the poem as a whole, and your sense of the writer
    so far*

Like 'The Voice', 'The Darkling Thrush' is an effective poem
which takes an old theme and gives it fresh life. At the heart of the
poem is a tension between the gloom of winter and hope associated
with the thrush, but the choice of words and the skilfully controlled
structure of the poem make it an attractive work. The use of
imagery, in particular, enables Hardy to touch on large issues
within the small frame of the poem. Let me repeat the point I made
earlier about not looking for cryptic messages in poems. Students
sometimes feel that poems contain hidden meanings. Where this
misconception comes from is the fact that poets use imagery to talk
about one thing in terms of another thing, but this is not a code
that needs to be broken. The general meaning is the obvious
meaning; what the imagery does is extend the meaning, adding all
kinds of nuances and subtleties, and it can also connect the specific
theme of the poem with broader issues of order and disorder in life.

The sense of Hardy that is emerging is of a poet who takes familiar
themes but who can inject remarkable new life into them. I want to
look briefly at one more of his poems to see what, if anything, we
can add to that. This is **'At Castle Boterel'**:

> As I drive to the junction of lane and highway,
>     And the drizzle bedrenches the waggonette,
> I look behind at the fading byway,
>     And see on its slope, now glistening wet,
>         Distinctly yet
>
> Myself and a girlish form benighted
>     In dry March weather. We climb the road
> Beside a chaise. We had just alighted
>     To ease the sturdy pony's load
>         When he sighed and slowed.
>
> What we did as we climbed, and what we talked of
>     Matters not much, nor to what it led, –
> Something that life will not be balked of
>     Without rude reason till hope is dead,
>         And feeling fled.

It filled but a minute. But was there ever
  A time of such quality, since or before,
In that hill's story? To one mind never,
    Though it has been climbed, foot-swift, foot-sore,
        By thousands more.

Primaeval rocks form the road's steep border,
  And much have they faced there, first and last,
Of the transitory in Earth's long order;
    But what they record in colour and cast
        Is – that we two passed.

And to me, though Time's unflinching rigour,
  In mindless rote, has ruled from sight
The substance now, one phantom figure
    Remains on the slope, as when that night
        Saw us alight.

I look and see it there, shrinking, shrinking,
  I look back at it amid the rain
For the very last time; for my sand is sinking,
    And I shall traverse old love's domain
        Never again.

1   *Look for a central opposition in the poem*

If we look for an opposition, we can say that the poem begins with
drizzle but Hardy looks beyond this to see himself and a girl in 'dry
March weather'. As against the miserable present is a happy
moment from the past. At heart, then, the poem seems little more
than a nostalgic recollection of happier days. If it does amount to
more than this is must be because Hardy adds some weight or
significance to his memory.

2   *Begin to look at the details of the poem, trying to see how the poet
    brings his theme to life*

The only way to discover how the poem does work is to start
analysing it, choosing a manageable section for closer examination.
The stanza I found most interesting is this one:

Primaeval rocks form the road's steep border,
　　And much have they faced there, first and last,
Of the transitory in Earth's long order;
　　But what they record in colour and cast
　　　　Is – that we two passed.

The first thing that strikes me here is that this is a complex sentence, and that its meaning is difficult to grasp. As I have explained earlier, however, we do not always need to understand difficult passages in poetry. Sometimes their difficulty itself tells us just about everything that we need to know. In this case, it is probably enough to grasp that some kind of statement is being made about the complicated nature of the passing of time. At the end of the stanza, however, things suddenly become very simple indeed in the startlingly clear phrase 'we two passed'. Can you see the effective way in which the affection of these two young people is placed and set against the whole involved history of the world and how it seems to illuminate a certain darkness?

3　*Look at another section of the poem, trying to see how the poem is progressing*

Part of the appeal of the poem is the simple way in which the young couple are described. When Hardy refers to 'Myself and a girlish form', they are real and tangible, whereas 'Time' is described in alienating terms: 'Time's unflinching rigour, / In mindless rote . . . '. This is true throughout the poem, that, whereas the language describing time is harsh and abstract, the language for the young couple is very plain. Whereas the thrush in the previous poem was associated with religious imagery, the language for the young couple is bare and free of wider associations:

It filled but a minute. But was there ever
　　A time of such quality, since or before,
In that hill's story?

The effect that Hardy seems to be aiming for is that the plain fact of boy-and-girl love should impress us by its simplicity amidst the more complex language the poem employs to talk about the other aspects of experience.

*4    Look at how the poem concludes*

We can see how Hardy is again exploiting the nature of language and its power to trigger off associations in our minds. On occasions, as is true here, the very fact of plain statement can be powerful. It is so, however, because it appears in the poem in the context of more elaborate language, a language that belongs to the world of maturity rather than youth. This becomes more evident at the end of the poem:

> And I shall traverse old love's domain
> > Never again.

There is something rather over-elaborate about the phrasing of the first line there, as if Hardy has become distanced, and his words have become distanced, from the simple but powerful fact of young love.

*5    Sum up your sense of the poem as a whole, and your sense of the writer so far*

As always with Hardy, it is the clever control of language that makes his poems come to life. Of course, the same could be said of every poet; it is the use of language that distinguishes a great poet from the mass of authors who just write as people have done before. In the case of Hardy, however, we particularly notice his craftsmanship because of the modesty of his poems. The poems are short and deal with everyday matters. His originality lies not in saying obviously new things but in injecting new life into those old themes. As such, however, Hardy's little poems often prove to be quite weighty poems as they turn so directly to the question of the importance of love in a world where death exists. What is most surprising is that many poets write short poems on domestic topics rather in the manner of Hardy, but nobody does as well as Hardy. In order to explain this it would perhaps be necessary to move outside the poems and start considering the fact that Hardy was writing at the end of the nineteenth century, and the special kind of relationship he therefore has to both romantic poetry and modern poetry. Such broader issues are, however, outside the scope of this book; it is the kind of question you might want to consider when you feel confident that you have come to terms with the characteristics of Hardy's verse and the essential qualities of how it works.

## Alexander Pope

One implication of the first half of this chapter has been that it is quite easy to talk about the technique of a poem. You need to know what you are looking for, principally in the areas of structure and imagery, and you also need to be alert to how the devices the poet employs add to the meaning of the poem. If you look for these things, you cannot go far wrong. The same method that works with Hardy will work well with all poets. All poets exploit the same repertoire of devices, and therefore it is always possible to look at language and structure in the kind of way I have described so far.

This should become apparent if we consider the work of a writer who is very unlike Hardy, the eighteenth-century poet Alexander Pope. One of the problems about discussing Pope is that many of his poems are very long – too long to be examined here as a whole in the way we have done so far; but we can work from small sections. It is, of course, essential that you read any poem as a whole first, but then you can start to build your view of the work from a passage such as the following from the **Epistle to Dr Arbuthnot**; it is a picture of a man called Sporus.

> Let Sporus tremble – 'What? that thing of silk,
> Sporus, that mere white curd of ass's milk?
> Satire or sense, alas! can Sporus feel?
> Who breaks a butterfly upon a wheel?'
> Yet let me flap this bug with gilded wings,
> This painted child of dirt, that stinks and stings;
> Whose buzz the witty and the fair annoys,
> Yet wit ne'er tastes, and beauty ne'er enjoys:
> So well-bred spaniels civilly delight
> In mumbling of the game they dare not bite.
> Eternal smiles his emptiness betray,
> As shallow streams run dimpling all the way.
> Whether in florid impotence he speaks,
> And, as the prompter breathes, the puppet squeaks;
> Or at the ear of Eve, familiar Toad,
> Half-froth, half-venom, spits himself abroad,

In puns, or politics, or tales, or lies,
Or spite, or smut, or rhymes, or blasphemies.
His wit all see-saw, between that and this,
Now high, now low, now Master up, now Miss,
And he himself one vile antithesis.
Amphibious thing! that acting either part,
The trifling head or the corrupted heart,
Fop at the toilet, flatterer at the board,
Now trips a lady, and now struts a lord.
Eve's tempter thus the rabbins have exprest,
A cherub's face, a reptile all the rest;
Beauty that shocks you, parts that none will trust;
Wit that can creep, and pride that licks the dust.

1   *Look for a central opposition in the poem*

If we can find an opposition in this passage it is likely to resemble
the opposition and theme evident in the poem as a whole. There is,
however, rather a lot of text to handle even in this extract, so it
might be better if we concentrate on just the first few lines:

> Let Sporus tremble – 'What? that thing of silk,
> Sporus, that mere white curd of ass's milk?
> Satire or sense, alas! can Sporus feel?
> Who breaks a butterfly upon a wheel?'

At first it might seem difficult to find a tension here. All we seem to
be offered is a portrait of an unattractive and unappealing man.
This comes across in the description of him as a 'thing of silk' and a
'mere white curd', and in the way that he is described as breaking
a butterfly upon a wheel. If you are unsure what to make of this,
you might feel tempted to look at the notes to try to find out who
Sporus was and whether he was based upon someone in real life.
This, however, is not important at this stage but is rather something
you can turn to later. At the outset you need to establish a sense of
an opposition and a theme. What I think must be evident is that
Sporus is a faulty character whose values are all wrong, so even
within these four lines we should be able to find some evidence of
alternative values endorsed by Pope. Pope's values are, in fact,
implicit in his angry denunciation of Sporus: Sporus is an extreme
and distasteful character, whereas Pope seems to uphold values of
moderation, balance and good sense.

2   *Begin to look at the details of the poem, trying to see how the poet brings his theme to life*

As the passage continues we should get a fuller picture of Sporus, and also a fuller sense of Pope's approved standards. Consider these lines, for example:

> Yet let me flap this bug with gilded wings,
> This painted child of dirt, that stinks and stings;
> Whose buzz the witty and the fair annoys,
> Yet wit ne'er tastes, and beauty ne'er enjoys . . . .

In essence Pope is saying, 'Here is an unpleasant man', but if we look at his use of language we can see how the idea is given extra force and meaning. As is always the case, poetic images carry rich associations; for example, the reference to Sporus as a 'painted child of dirt' manages to suggest a great deal, both in the idea of smearing face-paint over filth and in the implication of the effeminacy of a man who wears make-up. The central image in these few lines, however, is the association of Sporus with an insect; he is associated with something loathsome in nature, and indeed appears to be more of an animal or insect than a man. Such an image works at various levels. Most straightforwardly, it makes the picture of Sporus vivid and even amusing. The image also adds meaning to the poem, however, in the way it suggests Sporus's shortcomings, his less-than-human value, his contemptuousness. As always in great poetry, much more is being suggested about the nature of this man than is ever being directly stated. Beyond this, though, we can point to the way the image broadens the meaning of the poem by raising the whole larger issue of proper attitudes and values in life. It is the use of imagery, therefore, that makes this passage much more than just a venomous attack by Pope on Sporus (who was a contemporary of his called Lord Hervey) and turns it into a consideration of the broader questions of reasonable behaviour, corruption and perversion in life.

In order to appreciate this fully, however, we need to look at the other side of the opposition and see what standards Pope upholds. These lines we have been looking at suggest that one way of expressing Pope's values is to say that he upholds the concept of proper, manly behaviour, but if we look again at the lines we should be able to define his standards more fully. Think about the structure of the lines. We have already established that order, pattern and symmetry in verse suggest similar qualities in life, and the clearest thing about Pope's writing is just how disciplined and balanced the lines are. Take this example: 'Yet wit ne'er tastes, and beauty ne'er enjoys'. The two halves of the line mirror each other perfectly, and this helps suggest an idea of what Pope sees as good order. We can contrast this with the sort of movement associated with Sporus, who buzzes around like an insect. As against such mindless activity, Pope clearly stands for disciplined order, something that is reflected in his use of the rhyming couplet and how he imposes a strict, measured control all the time.

3   *Look at another section of the poem, trying to see how the poem is progressing*

My main points about how to discuss language and structure must be clear by now, so from this point on in this chapter my comments will be a lot briefer, just touching on issues and linking up points with the preceding chapters. If, then, we move forward in the Sporus passage, we come across these lines:

> . . . at the ear of Eve, familiar Toad,
> Half-froth, half-venom, spits himself abroad,
> In puns, or politics, or tales, or lies,
> O spite, or smut, or rhymes, or blasphemies.
> His wit all see-saw, between this and this,
> Now high, now low, now Master up, now Miss,
> And he himself one vile antithesis.

It is always a good idea to search for the images in a passage: we have already seen how Sporus is associated with an insect; here, though, he is presented like the serpent in the Garden of Eden. This adds to our sense of Sporus as a vile man, but also broadens the issue so that the poem again moves beyond being just a character sketch and becomes a much wider consideration of the presence of evil in existence. The words of the poem work on us, creating these ideas and associations, but the structure, too, contributes to the meaning of the poem: there is always a strong contrast between the giddy see-saw movements of Sporus and the controlled discipline of Pope's verse.

4   *Look at how the poem concludes*

Pope's own balance is particularly evident in the closing couplet of this extract:

> Beauty that shocks you, parts that none will trust;
> Wit that can creep, and pride that licks the dust.

The lines state their meaning, but if they strike you as powerful it is because of Pope's artistry, the way in which the perfect order and symmetry in his own verse rebukes Sporus's lack of discipline and so lack of value.

5   *Sum up your sense of the poem as a whole, and your sense of the writer so far*

We have only looked at one section from the *Epistle to Dr Arbuthnot*, but we can now say quite a lot about the poem as a whole. We have acquired a full sense of how Pope looks at people's behaviour in society and sees corruption and evil, and we can also appreciate how he sees himself as a man possessed of a correct sense of values, who must criticise and condemn those who fall short of a moderate and sensible standard of behaviour.

There could be more that we need to add to that view of Pope, however, so at this point it makes sense to move on to another extract from another poem to add to our picture of this writer. Obviously, if you were just studying *The Epistle to Dr Arbuthnot* you would choose further extracts from it: the important point to remember is that as you examine each extract you are trying to go further, to build your view in more detail. This is what I shall be trying to do as I look at an extract from a poem called **The Rape of the Lock**, which tells the story of how a young man cuts off a lock of a young woman's hair at a social gathering. In this particular passage we see the young woman putting on her make-up before going out:

> And now, unveiled, the Toilet stands displayed,
> Each silver vase in mystic order laid.
> First, robed in white, the Nymph intent adores,

With head uncovered, the cosmetic powers.
A heavenly image in the glass appears,
To that she bends, to that her eyes she rears;
The inferior Priestess, at her altar's side,
Trembling, begins the sacred Rites of Pride.
Unnumbered treasures ope at once, and here
The various offerings of the world appear;
From each she nicely culls with curious toil,
And decks the Goddess with the glittering spoil.
This casket India's glowing gems unlocks,
And all Arabia breathes from yonder box.
The tortoise here and elephant unite,
Transformed to combs, the speckled and the white.
Here files of pins extend their shining rows,
Puffs, powders, patches, Bibles, billet-doux.
Now awful Beauty puts on all its arms;
The fair each moment rises in her charms,
Repairs her smiles, awakens every grace,
And calls forth all the wonders of her face . . . .

1   *Look for a central opposition in the poem*

What is being described is a young woman putting on her make-up
in front of the mirror, but the kind of language used suggests a
religious ceremony. That might seem puzzling, except that we are
almost certain to realise that Pope's tone is mocking; he is mocking
social affectations and social failings. By describing something so
trivial in such inflated terms, he draws attention to its triviality.
The implicit sense of Pope that comes across, therefore, is of a man
of superior good sense who can see the folly of others. This view of
Pope is consistent with the view we constructed from our
examination of his portrait of Sporus, but a difference on this
occasion seems to be that Pope is amused rather than angry. The
passage, however, is not just comic, and as usual it is the imagery
that complicates the meaning. The use of religious imagery serves
to mock the girl, but it also hints at a more serious theme by
suggesting that self-worship, in this society, has replaced a true
sense of religious values.

2   *Begin to look at the details of the poem, trying to see how the poet brings his theme to life*

Can you see how alertness to Pope's imagery has already begun to point to deeper implications and a larger reach within this apparently trivial episode? A look at a few more lines from the extract at this stage could add to that sense of the poem. Having established that the theme is false and true values, your examination of the words used in a few lines of the poem could show how they work to create an impression of things running to excess in society. All you would need to report on is an inflated, exaggerated quality in the language. As against this, you could show how Pope's own couplets are controlled and disciplined at all times. It is, then, a simple blend of things that you focus on in any passage from any poet; that is, on the ways in which the structure, the choice and combination of words, and the images, work to give substance to a straightforward opposition at the heart of the poem.

3   *Look at another section of the poem, trying to see how the poem is progressing*

As you move from passage to passage your sense of the poem might not be altering all that much, but a full appreciation of the poem will be steadily accumulating. Take these lines, for example:

> This casket India's glowing gems unlocks,
> And all Arabia breathes from yonder box.
> The tortoise here and elephant unite,
> Transformed to combs, the speckled and the white.
> Here files of pins extend their shining rows,
> Puffs, powders, patches, Bibles, billet-doux.

The passage is easy to talk about if all the time you keep in mind that there is a close association between what you are noticing in the form of the passage and the meaning of the passage. To start with, for example, there is a kind of giddy jumble of references here: which reaches its climax in the line 'Puffs, powders, patches, Bibles, billet-doux'. Bibles appear amidst all the ephemera of the dressing-table, but that sums up the problem, that people in this society have lost any sense of what is solid and central in existence. Every detail, every word and every line, makes an active contribution to the overall effect of the passage. You cannot, however, hope to follow up every word, so select those that interest you most, and try to relate them to your developing sense of the passage's theme. For example, when Pope writes about the tortoise shells and the elephant tusks being made into two kinds of comb, the meaning that is consistent with the theme we have discovered is that there is something wrong with a society that transforms what is natural into social artifacts in this excessive kind of way. The image, therefore, confirms our sense of the poem's theme, but also adds to our grasp of the meaning of the poem.

4   *Look at how the poem concludes*

The closing lines of this extract are

> Repairs her smiles, awakens every grace,
> And calls forth all the wonders of her face . . . .

We could again comment here on falseness, on how the lines draw attention to the gap between the projected image of the woman and the truth about her, but the point I want to take up is that these lines, like the description as a whole, are funny. They are so because any description of someone acting in an extreme or exaggerated way is funny, but the true power of the passage is that it is simultaneously serious and comic. Society has lost any sense of true values, but there is something absurd about the whole notion of social folly.

5   *Sum up your sense of the poem as a whole, and your sense of the writer so far*

Over the years I have read a lot of examination answers on Pope's poetry, and usually there has been one noticeable failing. Candidates can always see that Pope is for moderation and against excess, but, having stated that, most students seem at a loss, and simply repeat the same point over and over again. What I hope has become evident in this discussion of Pope, however, is that even a small amount of attention to how he puts his poems together will enable you to write a full and interesting answer about him. The moment you report on the use and effect of an image, or the moment you look at how one of Pope's couplets challenges disorder in society, then your answer will acquire substance and authority. And the final result will be a subtle and complex appreciation of Pope as a writer.

Remember, however, that you must always pull back to report on what you have managed to.prove. If I do this myself now, I can add to the sense of Pope that I had put together at the end of discussing the Sporus passage. At that point I had gained a sense of what Pope stood for and what he was against, but a look at a second extract has, to my mind, made me realise rather more clearly how Pope is a comic satiric writer, laughing at those who are misguided, hoping to laugh them out of their folly.


A look at one more passage should add yet further to this view. This time I have chosen an extract from *The Dunciad*, a very long poem by Pope in which he presents a vision of civilised society disappearing as it is taken over by dunces, confidence tricksters and scoundrels. In these lines he presents his vision of the final triumph of Dullness:

> In vain, in vain, – the all-composing hour
> Resistless falls: the Muse obeys the Power.
> She comes! She comes! The sable throne behold
> Of Night primaeval, and of Chaos old!
> Before her, Fancy's gilded clouds decay,
> And all its varying rainbows die away.
> Wit shoots in vain its momentary fires,
> The meteor drops, and in a flash expires,
> As one by one, at dread Medea's strain,
> The sickening stars fade off the ethereal plain;
> As Argus' eyes by Hermes' wand opprest,
> Closed one by one to everlasting rest;
> Thus at her felt approach, and secret might,
> Art after Art goes out, and all is Night.
> See skulking Truth to her old cavern fled,
> Mountains of Casuistry heaped o'er her head!
> Philosophy, that leaned on Heaven before,
> Shrinks to her second cause, and is no more.
> Physic of Metaphysic begs defence,
> And Metaphysic calls for aid on Sense!
> See Mystery to Mathematics fly!
> In vain! They gaze, turn giddy, rave and die.

Religion blushing veils her sacred fires,
And unawares Morality expires.
Nor public Flame, nor private, dares to shine;
Nor human Spark is left, nor Glimpse divine!
Lo! thy dread Empire, Chaos, is restored;
Light dies before thy uncreating word:
Thy hand, great Anarch, lets the curtain fall;
And Universal Darkness buries All.

1   *Look for a central opposition in the poem*

We can start with the opening four lines of this extract:

> In vain, in vain, – the all-composing hour
> Resistless falls: the Muse obeys the Power.
> She comes! She comes! The sable throne behold
> Of Night primaeval, and of Chaos old!

The subject matter is the advent of chaos and the night, yet the
lines in which this is described are perfectly balanced. The tension,
therefore, is between chaos and order, with the concept of order
being built into the very texture of the verse.

2   *Begin to look at the details of the poem, trying to see how the poet
    brings his theme to life*

The obvious thing we have to report on in the language of the
poem is how Pope manages to create a picture of chaos, how he
manages to convey a sense of the triumph of Dullness. We could
talk about a kind of inflated grandeur that Pope creates in these
lines, but as is often the case we are likely to make most progress if
we focus immediately on the use of imagery. The kind of imagery
we should need to investigate in this passage is the cosmic imagery,
which manages to suggest the enormous scale of the disorder that is
about to destroy civilisation. But this is not the only line of
imagery; another line, that is perhaps inevitable in a sequence like
this, is the triumph of darkness over light. As always, such images
bring the theme to life, but also add to and broaden the meaning of
the poem.

3   *Look at another section of the poem, trying to see how the poem is progressing*

I have selected some lines from just over half way through the extract:

> Philosophy, that leaned on Heaven before,
> Shrinks to her second cause, and is no more.
> Physic of Metaphysic begs defence,
> And Metaphysic calls for aid on Sense!
> See Mystery to Mathematics fly!
> In vain! They gaze, turn giddy, rave and die.

The imagery now is of different intellectual disciplines, such as philosophy and mathematics. The point being made is that all these have collapsed into some kind of giddy mess. The actual movement of the lines helps suggest this state of confusion, but this is only secondary to the words in the lines, and how they add to our sense of disorder taking over and destroying all intellectual effort.

4   *Look at how the poem concludes*

I have said before in this book that there will be some alteration in the balance of the tension at the end of a poem. This is also evident at the end of this passage, for now there is a total triumph of darkness:

> Lo! thy dread Empire, Chaos, is restored!
> Light dies before thy uncreating word:
> Thy hand, great Anarch, lets the curtain fall;
> And Universal Darkness buries All.

What I find most interesting here is that Pope is offering an extremely ambitious vision of the triumph of disorder, yet the technique he relies on, even at a point such as this, is one of the most basic techniques of poetry: the lines are dominated by light and dark imagery. This underlines one of the points I have been making throughout this chapter, which is that even the most ambitious or original poetry is constructed out of familiar materials.

5   *Sum up your sense of the poem as a whole, and your sense of the writer
so far*

There is just one point I still need to settle in my discussion of
Pope. On a number of occasions in this book I have dismissed the
idea that poetry has 'a message', but Pope's poetry might seem to
contradict this in so far as it seems obviously didactic. He seems
poised and confident, perfectly in control, and astute in his
understanding of the shortcomings of others. This passage from *The
Dunciad* does, however, make me wonder about that 'neat' view of
Pope. Can he really be so confident when he sees chaos as
imminent? Is it really a sense of Pope's ordered values that emerges
from the passage, or a sense of terrible disorder in society? Pope
certainly does not have the answer to society's problems, and,
indeed, such an irrational society is likely to take little heed of his
advice. What this suggests is that, instead of Pope being simply a
poet of sane and ordered values, there is a wavering instability in
his verse as he presents a vision of disorder and plays with a notion
of order, but realises that the gap between the two will remain
unbridgeable. This is a view of the kind of tension in poetry that I
have touched on throughout this book, particularly in the discussion
of Keats, but it will become far more central in the next chapter,
which deals with the subject of difficult poetry.

Before moving on, however, let me pause to take stock of what
general lessons about how to discuss poetry have developed in this
chapter. Everything I have said is essentially an extension of the
earlier chapters: that is, that you need to be able to get hold of the
theme of a poem quickly, and then look at how this theme is
brought to life. The poet's use of imagery is absolutely central in
his making of a poem; imagery is not just poetic decoration but
something that adds to and broadens the meaning of a poem.
Imagery is, however, not the only thing that needs to be discussed.
I have kept on returning to imagery in this chapter, but the best
approach, once you have established your broad view, is simply to
take a few lines from the poem and comment on whatever seems
most significant to you in those lines. At first this can seem difficult,
but, the moment you realise that the lines in question must be
offering a small-scale reflection of the concerns of the poem as a
whole, then you have the key that enables you to unlock and
explore a poem.

# 4

# Difficult poetry

I HAVE suggested so far in this book that analysing poetry is a fairly straightforward matter, and up to a point this is true. It is easy to spot a central theme in a poem and easy to see at least some of the ways in which the poet brings his or her theme to life. Looking closely at the words on the page is bound to result in a keener understanding of both the poem and the broader characteristics of the poet's work. There might be occasions when you feel that your progress is slow, but the more you practice analysing poetry the more confident you will become. There might be times, however, when you feel that you are getting nowhere, times when you feel unable to make any progress because of the difficulty of the poems that you are trying to analyse.

There is a sense in which all poetry is difficult. Every poet uses language in a concentrated way to convey experiences, emotions and ideas. When we read a poem, we are not confronted by a plain statement. Language is being used in an evocative and associative way, with the result that the poem is likely to suggest far more than it ever directly states. This fact, that a poem does not directly state its meaning, is the fundamental thing that makes poetry, and the analysis of poetry, difficult. We have to commit ourselves, we have to offer ideas about what lines of a poem might mean, and in doing so we run the risk of misreading the poem. I hope that the method of analysis I have been describing will help you spot the broad significance of a poem, so avoiding total misinterpretation of the work, but interpretation of individual images can be more problematic. An example should make this plain. This is a stanza from 'Dejection: An Ode' by Samuel Taylor Coleridge:

> My genial spirits fail;
> And what can these avail
> To lift the smothering weight from off my breast?
> It were a vain endeavour,

Though I should gaze for ever
On that green light that lingers in the west:
I may not hope from outward forms to win
The passion and the life, whose fountains are within.

We can, if we look for an opposition, arrive without too much trouble at a sense of the theme of this poem. Coleridge is feeling dejected; what he seeks is happiness. In the course of this stanza he makes it clear that it is vain to hope that some external stimulus will cheer him up; the change has to come from within. All of this is stated fairly directly. We can see that Coleridge is presenting a standard poetic tension, the tension between feelings of unhappiness and the desire for joy. There are no problems so far, then, but problems do appear as soon as we take a closer look at the words, for example at the phrase 'that green light that lingers in the west'. What does this mean? No precise meaning is stated, and different readers are likely to respond to the line in different ways. To me, for example, the word 'green' ties up with the idea of nature, and I am also struck by the contrast between light in this image and Coleridge's dark feelings elsewhere in the poem. Other readers, however, might take other impressions from the line. And this is the constant difficulty of poetry, that more is being suggested than is ever directly stated, and that you as a reader have to commit yourself to a view of the significance of phrases and images in a poem. You might well feel hesitant about committing yourself in this way, but if you proceed methodically, searching for sensible implications of the imagery which are in line with your developing sense of the poem as a whole, then you should be able to do justice to the poem you are analysing.

There is, then, this sense in which all poetry is difficult, but there is some poetry that is difficult in a rather different way. There are poets who deliberately write in a difficult manner so that what they say becomes hard to follow; as readers, we find ourselves unable to follow the sense of a long involved sentence, or we might feel that the stanzas or sections of a poem barely relate to each other. Poets who employ tactics such as these are writing in a way that must be intended to make reading the poem hard work. I look at two such writers in this chapter, John Donne and T. S. Eliot. What I have to say about them, however, might help you with any writer whose stanzas and sentences are convoluted and involved, and with any poems where the basic meaning is hard to make out.

This kind of difficulty is in some ways, however, only a surface difficulty in verse. The true subject of this chapter is the difficulty that can be said to be at the heart of all great poetry, which is the weight of meaning that can be conveyed in even a short poem. The problem for us as readers is doing justice to the subtleties and nuances of such works. Great poems can seem endlessly to evade our grasp as critics as we attempt to pin them down but then realise that the meaning of the poem is more complex than we have realised so far. In one way, what I am talking about here is what I was talking about at the start of this chapter, which is the ability of poetry to suggest more than it directly says, but my more particular focus in this chapter is the kind of open quality that there is in great poetry, where we feel that any order being established in the verse is very precarious. As critics, we always seem to be taking too neat and packaged a view of the nature and effect of the verse. When we discuss the works of the greatest poets, we almost inevitably feel that we are trying to define something that evades definition. As I try to show in the following pages, however, the simple approach we have followed so far should help us to get as close as it is possible to get to capturing the essence of even the most ambitious writers.

## John Donne

The obvious problem with Donne is that his poems are hard to read and hard to understand. In order to cope with his verse we have to choose between two approaches, of which the one is short-sighted and the other requires us to think for ourselves. The mistaken approach would be to find out, say from a critical book, what Donne's poetry is 'all about' and then look at his poems in the light of these ideas. The much more rewarding approach is to build a view of Donne from the evidence of a few of his poems, and that, obviously, is the method I shall illustrate here. I start with **'The Sun Rising'**: do not worry if you cannot understand it. There is nothing wrong with your response; indeed it is in some ways the correct response, as Donne has deliberately written a poem that is taxing to follow.

> Busy old fool, unruly Sun,
>     Why dost thou thus,
> Through windows, and through curtains call on us?

Must to thy motions lovers' seasons run?
      Saucy pedantic wretch, go chide
      Late school-boys, and sour prentices,
    Go tell Court-huntsmen, that the King will ride,
    Call country ants to harvest offices;
Love, all alike, no season knows, nor clime,
Nor hours, days, months, which are the rags of time.

      Thy beams, so reverend, and strong
        Why shouldst thou think?
I could eclipse and cloud them with a wink,
But that I would not lose her sight so long:
      If her eyes have not blinded thine,
      Look, and tomorrow late, tell me,
    Whether both th' Indias of spice and Mine
Be where thou left'st them, or lie here with me.
Ask for those Kings whom thou saw'st yesterday,
And thou shalt hear, All here in one bed lay.

      She's all States, and all Princes, I,
        Nothing else is.
Princes do but play us; compared to this,
All honour's mimic; all wealth alchemy.
      Thou sun art half as happy as we,
      In that the world's contracted thus;
    Thine age asks ease, and since thy duties be
    To warm the world, that's done in warming us.
Shine here to us, and thou art everywhere;
This bed thy centre is, these walls thy sphere.

1   *Look for a central opposition in the poem*

This poem starts abruptly, and as soon as it starts there is a rapid
sequence of images which accumulate so quickly that it is difficult
to take them all in. It is difficult to spot a theme because these
surface details are so bewildering. What we must do, however, is
look behind the surface in order to establish a sense of the basic
theme of the poem. We can concentrate on the first few lines:

    Busy old fool, unruly Sun,
      Why dost thou thus,
Through windows, and through curtains call on us?
Must to thy motions lovers' seasons run?

The only thing I can get hold of here is the mention of love, but this should prove enough to get started. Love is repeatedly presented in poetry as something positive in a bewildering or dark world; it seems reasonable to assume, therefore, that love is going to be put forward in this poem as something important in a disordered world. And, indeed, the sun is called 'unruly' in the first line, as if Donne wants to get away from the unruliness of life and retreat into a secure existence with his love. It is a variation on a familiar theme of love versus the world.

2    *Begin to look at the details of the poem, trying to see how the poet brings his theme to life*

It is reassuring to know that familiar themes are at the heart of even the most complex poems. What we are really interested in, however, is what Donne does with this theme. The best way to start discovering this is to select a few lines for close attention. In this instance, I have picked some more lines from the first stanza, as Donne continues to address the sun:

> Saucy pedantic wretch, go chide
> Late school-boys, and sour prentices,
> Go tell Court-huntsmen, that the King will ride,
> Call country ants to harvest offices;
> Love, all alike, no season knows, nor clime,
> Nor hours, days, months, which are the rags of time.

Donne continues to praise love and to scorn the sun. This is apparent in the disrespectful way that he addresses the sun as a 'Saucy pedantic wretch', and in the way he elevates love as knowing 'no season . . . , nor clime . . . ', as if it is above all the instability of the world. What, however, do the other lines contribute to the poem? One point is that the images broaden the issue. Donne writes about schoolboys and apprentices and then about the court; such concrete images make us see how the sun organises every area of life. Yet Donne elevates the private order of love above the wider order of the world as symbolised by the sun. When he criticises the sun he uses words such as 'fool', 'unruly' and 'saucy', all of which suggest disorderly behaviour. The truth is, however, that the sun orders and organises the whole of existence. What we can see in all of this is a playful streak in Donne's poetry. Many poets might set love against the gloomy waste of existence,

but Donne takes an irreverent delight in setting the power of love
against the power of the sun.

3    *Look at another section of the poem, trying to see how the poem is
     progressing*

So far I have spotted something about Donne's poetry – its playful
quality – but do not know what to make of that insight. The best
way to make progress is simply to return to the poem, hoping that
the evidence of the text will show me where to go next. The
opening of the second stanza should prove as revealing as any other
section of the poem:

> Thy beams, so reverend, and strong
> > Why shouldst thou think?
> I could eclipse and cloud them with a wink,
> But that I would not lose her sight so long . . . .

Thematically, these lines present no problem: they continue and
develop the idea of the power of love versus the power of the sun.
What is perplexing, however, is the ingenuity and playfulness –
apparent, for example, in the way that the idea of an eclipse of the
sun is turned inside out so that Donne's eye eclipses the sun by
winking. He is reluctant to wink, though, for he does not want to
lose sight of his love for even so short a space of time. We can see
that Donne delights in playing with ideas, but need to find some
justification for his inventiveness; we need to determine how the
technique employed in the poem affects the meaning of the poem.

We might make some progress if we turn again to ideas about
poetry that I have already presented in this book. I have written
about how poets search for order in a disordered universe; they do
this by looking for connections and establishing links between
images. At times they can create a sense of harmony and stillness
in existence. Donne's approach, however, where he takes images,
turns them inside out, and plays with them, seems to pull in the
opposite direction, creating a sense of a mobile and confusing
world. The sun might traditionally suggest warmth, security and
order, but when Donne's mind gets to work on the subject the
result is a restless, and often rather unnerving, view of things. We
can, I think, relate this to some of the characteristics that are
always in evidence in Donne's poetry; there are rapid leaps in
imagery, twisting of ideas, and the turning inside out of all kinds of

concepts. All of this suggests a giddy world which it is difficult to get the measure of. In 'The Sun Rising' we know that the sun represents the natural order, but almost immediately we are aware of a kind of chaos in existence. Donne's tone, where we never quite know whether he is being serious or not, contributes to the sense of uncertainty in the poem. Nothing seems secure, reliable or trustworthy; the poet is talking to us, but frequently we do not know whether he is serious or tongue-in-cheek. All of this effectively contributes to the sense of the bewildering nature of existence.

### 4    *Look at how the poem concludes*

The techniques Donne employs are very sophisticated: he has to be able to dash from idea to idea, to play with images, and speak in a rather ambiguous voice. In a way, the effect of these techniques is very simple, for they all work to create the sense of a rather bewildering world, where any sense of order is going to be difficult to pin down. What can be hung on to, however, is love; either divine love or, as in this poem, human love. It comes as no great surprise, therefore, that love is triumphant at the end of 'The Sun Rising' as Donne again addresses the sun:

> and since thy duties be
>   To warm the world, that's done in warming us.
> Shine here to us, and thou art everywhere;
> This bed thy centre is, these walls thy sphere.

At the beginning love was in competition with the sun, and throughout the poem there has been a tension between the two, but, as often happens at the end of a poem, the original opposition is resolved or seen in a new light; what happens here is that the sun is made part of the lovers' scheme of things, a scheme of things which is summed up in the last line when their bed becomes the centre of an ordered universe.

At one level, then, there are no problems here: we have identified a tension, and seen how the poem resolves the tension, by making love triumphant. We might, however, be wary of the tone and method of this resolution. It is suspiciously clever and ingenious; it is as if the poem has been a cryptic puzzle and Donne has finally worked out a contrived answer. Again, then, any problems we feel about Donne are really due to this playfulness and cleverness that always characterises his verse. Indeed, some readers, on the basis of the evidence so far, might dismiss Donne as an intellectual poet who is deficient in the areas of honesty and feeling. To my mind, however, what is in evidence again here is Donne's sense of the complex and bewildering nature of existence; the self-conscious artifice of the closing lines of this poem serves to draw attention to the questionable nature of any ordered certainties that mankind might try to create in a bewildering world. At the end of the poem, therefore, we are left, not so much with a sense of love as triumphant, as with a sense of the confusing, complex nature of experience.

5  *Sum up your sense of the poem as a whole, and your sense of the writer so far*

Perhaps the simplest way of expressing the points I have made so far is to talk about the very close correspondence between form and content. A Donne poem is difficult and bewildering and even exhausting to read. We should, therefore, be wary of tidying it up and reducing it to a neat meaning. We are falsifying the poem if we place too much emphasis on its positive notion of love. The words which in fact best describe the content of the poem are those that we might use to talk about its form: that the poem is intent on offering a sense of a difficult, bewildering and exhausting world. And all Donne's techniques are employed to project this sense of experience.

These comments on 'The Sun Rising' might well point to the heart of the problem, not only with Donne but also with all difficult poets. Where we are likely to go wrong with Donne is if we try to tidy him up too much, if, for example, we say that he praises the importance of love in a disordered world. This reading seems wrong because it does not pay sufficient attention to the hectic complexity of the texture of his verse. What we need to do is look at, and appreciate, how he manages to create a sense of the immense complexity of existence. And probably what all the greatest poets have in common is an ability to convey a sense of life's complexity. They will employ techniques that differ from Donne's, but the result will always be that we feel an infinite sense of the disorder of life. But a sense of disorder alone is not enough: there must be some attempt to order and control, and Donne's mental gymnastics testify ably to the important impulse in mankind to try to confront and make some sense of a confusing world.

This is again something that can be said about all the finest poetry: we feel that such poetry does justice to the complexity of experience, yet also reflects the need to create order and significance in a bewildering world. But too confident an order would strike us as trite or sentimental. There is something breathtaking about the finest poetry, where any control that emerges seems precarious, and where there is a constant sense of everything just about to collapse or fall apart. And this is part of the difficulty in writing about good poetry, that you have to be alert to how it is pulling in two directions at the same time, that it is acknowledging the disorder of experience but also playing with the possibilities of order. The most common fault in studying poetry is making too much of a positive 'message' in a writer, and not acknowledging the trembling, wavering instability of very good writing. In the case of Donne, it is necessary to be alert to the complicating techniques he employs, and to understand how such techniqes suggest not only a giddy world but also a desire to confront that giddy world.

If all this is still very vague, a look at another Donne poem might make things clearer. This time I have chosen **'The Anniversary'**:

> All Kings, and all their favourites,
>     All glory of honours, beauties, wits,
> The Sun itself, which makes times, as they pass,
> Is elder by a year, now, than it was
> When thou and I first one another saw:
> All other things, to their destruction draw,
>     Only our love hath no decay;
> This, no tomorrow hath, nor yesterday,
> Running it never runs from us away,
> But truly keeps his first, last, everlasting day.

> Two graves must hide thine and my corse,
>     If one might, death were no divorce,
> Alas, as well as other Princes, we,
> (Who Prince enough in one another be,)
> Must leave at last in death, these eyes, and ears,
> Oft fed with true oaths, and with sweet salt tears;
>     But souls where nothing dwells but love
> (All other thoughts being inmates) then shall prove

This, or a love increased there above,
When bodies to their graves, souls from their graves remove.

And then we shall be thoroughly blessed,
    But we no more, than all the rest.
Here upon earth, we're Kings, and none but we
Can be such Kings, nor of such subjects be;
Who is so safe as we? where none can do
Treason to us, except one of us two.
    True and false fears let us refrain,
Let us love nobly, and live, and add again
Years and years unto years, till we attain
To write threescore: this is the second of our reign.

1   *Look for a central opposition in the poem*

If we look at the opening lines of this poem, it is again clear that
love is at the centre of things, and, as in 'The Sun Rising', love is
being set against the world. Everything is older by a year, but their
love has remained constant. It is a very familiar theme: we are
presented with ideas of waste and destruction, yet love represents
something to hold on to in such a disordered world. The words of
the poem reveal the theme, but Donne's handling of line structure
is also important. The poem starts with a long, involved sentence
about the passing of time. As against this, there is the simplicity of
'Only our love hath no decay': love is simple, and a simply
expressed value, in a complex world. Things would, of course, be
simple if we could leave them there, but, as always in a Donne
poem, he will not allow us the luxury of a steady and relaxed view.
This becomes evident at the end of the first stanza, where, having
introduced the concept of love in a neat, self-contained line, he
starts to pursue the concept, telling us that love

        no tomorrow hath, nor yesterday,
    Running it never runs from us away,
    But truly keeps his first, last, everlasting day.

There is a gap between the idea and the expression of the idea. All
that is being said is that love is reliable, still and unchanging, but
then Donne's playfulness takes over; suddenly there is a sense that
love is not the simple answer he has suggested it is, but an elusive

concept. The structure of these lines, where he seems to tie himself up in knots trying to explain love, dramatically undercuts the neat certainty of 'Only our love hath no decay'.


2    *Begin to look at the details of the poem, trying to see how the poet brings his theme to life*

As in 'The Sun Rising', Donne has taken a familiar theme, and seems to be developing a familiar tension between the disorder of experience and the order of love. His slipperiness as a poet, however, undercuts the easy answer. Once again we are thrown back on the confusing nature of experience, and made to feel that any concept of order is precarious and far from simple. A simple poet might say that life is awful, but love redeems the horror of it all: in Donne, however, we are made to feel the complexity of experience and not allowed the consolation of easy answers. If, though, we are to do justice to the poem, we need to look at how Donne creates such a sense of complexity in his writing.

We can turn to the opening of the second stanza:

> Two graves must hide thine and my corse,
>   If one might, death were no divorce,
> Alas, as well as other Princes, we,
> (Who Prince enough in one another be,)
> Must leave at last in death, these eyes, and ears
> Oft fed with true oaths, and with sweet salt tears . . . .

The idea, in these very convoluted lines, is that their love will last for ever, for even if they die their souls in heaven will continue to be in love. We cannot, though, ignore the manner in which the idea is expressed, and, as is often the case with poetry, the best way of talking about the content of the lines is to use the words that best describe their formal characteristics. These lines, for example, strike me as involved and hard to understand, so what they mainly suggest to me is just how hard it is to understand a fact such as death and a concept such as love; tying things up in knots itself suggests the knotted nature of experience.

But Donne does not simply want to lose and confuse us, even though his lines about love might seem very confusing. This second stanza concludes

> But souls where nothing dwells but love
> (All other thoughts being inmates) then shall prove
> This, or a love increased there above,
> When bodies to their graves, souls from their graves remove.

He is again talking of a love that endures beyond death and bodily decay, but it is again the difficulty of the lines that is most apparent. They seem to throw us back on the bewildering nature of everything. Yet the struggle to understand, and construct sentences that confront the complex facts, is also important, for the struggle of the sentences dramatises the need there is to understand experience. Other people might write more direct love poetry, but this poem manages to convey to us both a sense of the world and how we try to cope with the world. What is enacted in the form of the poem, in the way that the words wrestle with the world, is to a large extent the meaning of the poem.

3   *Look at another section of the poem, trying to see how the poem is progressing*

What makes Donne's poetry so complex all the time is his playful, ingenious approach. His ingenuity is particularly apparent at the opening of the third stanza:

> And then we shall be throughly blessed,
> But we no more, than all the rest.
> Here upon earth, we're Kings, and none but we
> Can be such Kings, nor of such subjects be;
> Who is so safe as we? where none can do
> Treason to us, except one of us two.

Characteristics of this poem that we have seen already are again in evidence. The first line is neat and self-contained: 'And then we shall be throughly blessed': it suggests the peace that the couple will know after death. But the following lines disrupt this idea, finding all kinds of niggles in this apparent solution. This reveals Donne's way of always disrupting neat ideas: the moment he offers an ordered vision, he immediately picks holes in it. The restlessness of his mind is apparent as he flits off to images of kings and treason. It is exhausting poetry to read, as we are not allowed to relax: as readers, we like to get hold of things and pin them down, but

Donne will not allow us that comfort. And his playfulness of tone contributes to that: we do not know where we are with this voice, we do not know whether he is serious or joking, but that ambiguous tone of voice is in line with all the other disorienting features in Donne's verse.

### 4    *Look at how the poem concludes*

When the initial tension is love versus the world, we expect love to dominate at the end of a poem. Let us look, therefore, at how 'The Anniversary' ends:

> Let us love nobly, and live, and add again
> Years and years unto years, till we attain
> To write threescore: this is the second of our reign.

Superficially this seems simple: the directness of a concept such as 'Let us love nobly' is obvious. But then other things happen to the sentence. As it goes on, Donne adding several phrases, the simplicity of the concept is undercut. Donne is again undermining a simple notion of love. This is particularly apparent in the way that he starts dating his previously timeless concept of love: love now cannot be separated off from time and change.

### 5    *Sum up your sense of the poem as a whole, and your sense of the writer so far*

As Donne is a difficult poet, I am aware that sections of this chapter might be hard to follow, so let me try to spell out as straightforwardly as possible what I think I have established so far. Donne uses familiar poetic tensions. In particular he sets love against the complexity and disorder of the world. The techniques he employs as a poet, such as flitting from idea to idea, ingenious imagery, and playing with concepts, all suggest the diverse and complex nature of the world. He does not, however, have any simple answers: when he starts to develop love as a counterforce to the mess of experience, he soon confronts all the contradictions and puzzles in the concept of love. His playful tone of voice contributes to our sense of being confused. Yet we come away from the poetry with something more than just a sense of the bewildering complexity of experience, for the very ingenuity and inventiveness of the verse suggest the way in which mankind uses its intellect to try to make sense of the world. There is, therefore, always a wavering, unstable balance between disorder and order in Donne's poetry. What makes it so hard to sum up our sense of Donne is that we do not know how to strike a balance. We are likely to make too much of his sense of disorder, or too much of his sense of order as seen in love; or, if we try to do justice to both, we are awkwardly aware that the balance is more unstable than we have managed to express. And what is true of Donne is, I think, true of all great poetry, that its meanings are created within the space between awareness of the disorder of experience and the desire to find an order in existence.

In turning to a third Donne poem, what we need to pursue is this instability in his verse; we need to pursue the way in which he writes so that we can see how his poems can suggest both the diversity of experience and a need for pattern. Other great poets will also reveal a similar tension in their work, but every great poet will have his own way of bringing this to life. Donne's own way should become further evident in our third example, **'The Canonisation'**:

> For God's sake hold your tongue, and let me love,
>     Or chide my palsy, or my gout,
> My five grey hairs, or ruined fortune flout,
>         With wealth your state, your mind with arts improve,
>             Take you a course, get you a place,
>             Observe his honour, or his grace,
>     And the King's real, or his stamped face
>         Contemplate; what you will, approve,
>         So you will let me love.
>
> Alas, alas, who's injured by my love?
>     What merchant's ships have my sighs drowned?
> Who says my tears have overflowed his ground?
>         When did my colds a forward spring remove?
>             When did the heats which my veins fill
>             Add one more to the plaguy bill?
> Soldiers find wars, and Lawyers find out still
>         Litigious men, which quarrels move,
>         Though she and I do love.

Call us what you will, we're made such by love;
    Call her one, me another fly,
We're Tapers too, and at our own cost die,
    And we in us find the Eagle and the Dove;
        The Phoenix riddle hath more wit
        By us; we two being one, are it.
So to one neutral thing both sexes fit
    We die and rise the same, and prove
    Mysterious by this love.

We can die by it, if not live by love,
    And if unfit for tombs and hearse
Our legend be, it will be fit for verse;
    And if no piece of Chronicle we prove,
        We'll build in sonnets pretty rooms;
        As well a well-wrought urn becomes
The greatest ashes, as half-acre tombs,
    And by these hymns, all shall approve
    Us Canonised for love;

And thus invoke us: 'You whom reverend love
    Made one another's hermitage;
You, to whom love was peace, that now is rage;
    Who did the whole world's soul contract, and drove
        Into the glasses of your eyes
        (So made such mirrors, and such spies,
That they did all to you epitomise,)
    Countries, Towns, Courts: Beg from above
    A pattern of your love!'

1   *Look for a central opposition in the poem*

Love is again central. Love is presented as the important thing, and all the concerns of the world are dismissed. Donne does not care for ambition; he just wants to be left alone to devote himself to love.

2   *Begin to look at the details of the poem, trying to see how the poet brings his theme to life*

Donne, as always, starts in full flow, and then bombards us with images; this approach quickly establishes a sense of the busy, giddy nature of the world. In the second stanza he develops the idea of an opposition between love and the world:

> Alas, alas, who's injured by my love?
>   What merchant's ships have my sighs drowned?
> Who says my tears have overflowed his ground?
>   When did my colds a forward spring remove?

Donne's use of imagery, in particular the images of merchant's ships and land, starts to establish a fuller sense of a whole diverse world of commerce and activity. Yet there is an undercurrent of a tension all the time, for in every line there is a reference to Donne the lover who wants to be left alone by this wider world. So far, however, the poem is not all that difficult, for there is a very controlled division between Donne and the world: the world goes its own way, and the lovers just want to be in love. The images have suggested the diversity of the world, but, so far, Donne has not really started to tie things up in knots or juggled with concepts.

3   *Look at another section of the poem, trying to see how the poem is progressing*

This changes, however, as the third stanza begins; what signals this to us is simply the fact that the poem suddenly becomes much harder to understand.

> Call us what you will, we're made such by love;
>   Call her one, me another fly,
> We're Tapers too, and at our own cost die,
>   And we in us find the Eagle and the Dove . . . .

The source of the difficulty here is Donne's use of metaphors of flies and tapers to describe their love. In so far as I can understand it, Donne appears to be saying that he and his love are like two flies, but they are also two candles. Somehow they die when they fly into the candle-flame, but also survive. It seems to be a kind of reconciliation of opposites within themselves, such as when they are aware of the extremes of the eagle and the dove within themselves. But, even if we cannot quite understand what Donne is saying, we can ask why he introduces such strange metaphors.

There is, in fact, a term for metaphors of this kind where

comparisons are established between things which seem to have no obvious similarity or connection: the term is 'conceits'. The term means comparing two very dissimilar things from dissimilar areas of experience. The comparison can seem far-fetched, such as when Donne compares lovers to flies and candles. The widespread use of conceits is one of the major characteristics of Donne's poetry, but one that often causes confusion. The standard examination explanation of conceits is that initially they strike us as strange but on reflection they seem appropriate. The thing about conceits, however, is that we should not look all that far beyond the initial impression of finding the comparison ingenious and strained. The conceit is meant to make us feel how wide and varied the world is, and that it is only by the utmost ingenuity that connections can be established in such a diffuse world. This is particularly true when Donne employs the kind of conceit where, as on one occasion, he compares lovers and a pair of compasses. How, we might well ask, do you make sense of and establish connections in a world where things as different as love and compasses exist? But, just as a conceit suggests the complexity of the world, it also enacts the poet's desire to make connections, to establish links, to strive for some kind of understanding of the world, even if the signs of strain show.

The conceit, in miniature, sums up the kind of double impulse I have been writing about that exists in Donne's poetry. On the one hand it acknowledges the complex variety of experience, but on the other it reflects the poet's need to establish connections. Yet we are aware of something strained and precarious in the connections established; this in itself, however, merely reinforces a sense of the desperate need mankind has to try to make sense of the world. We feel the poet's impulse to understand and explain, but we also feel the poet's acknowledgement that it is perhaps only poetic ingenuity that can see an order in things.

### 4    *Look at how the poem concludes*

As the poem goes on, love remains central, but we might also suspect that it is only poetic cleverness that is keeping it central. The same indeterminacy of meaning is maintained as Donne writes about how they will be made holy figures who have been 'canonised for love'. This is sustained in the last stanza. At first it seems a simple celebration of the lovers as holy figures:

And thus invoke us: 'You whom reverend love
  Made one another's hermitage;
You, to whom love was peace, that now is rage;
  Who did the whole world's soul contract, and drove
    Into the glasses of your eyes
    (So made such mirrors, and such spies,
That they did all to you epitomise,)
    Countries, Towns, Courts: Beg from above
    A pattern of your love!'

The straightforward meaning is that they are to be worshipped as lovers, for they provide a pattern for the world. Originally the tension was love versus the world, but now love is triumphant as they are presented as holy figures who inspire the world. The problem, however, is that this idea is rather far-fetched, as is the whole conceit of establishing a connection between these lovers and saints. But again we can see the conceit pulling both ways: the difference between human lovers and sainthood suggests the complexity of the world, but the poet's linking of the secular and the divine through a conceit suggests the desire to make sense of the world. Yet the very ingenuity of the connection enables Donne to acknowledge that there is something strained in any attempt to perceive such an order in experience.

5   *Sum up your sense of the poem as a whole, and your sense of the writer so far*

Different poets employ different techniques and have their own distinctive views of the world, but the kind of unstable and unresolved tension that I have described in Donne's poetry is evident in much of the finest poetry. The poet is torn between a sense of the complexity of experience and a desire to find meaning and significance in experience. One kind of fairly weak poet might just overwhelm us with a sense of life's disorder; a more common kind of weak poet could impose excessively simple patterns upon experience, perhaps finding a glib sentimental lesson in the experience described. A good poet, however, manages to suggest both the diversity of life and the endless wrestle with words to try to make sense of life. It is this idea of the open rather than closed quality of difficult poetry that I am principally concerned to explore in this chapter. That is why I do not want to explore Donne any further here. There is much more that could be said; in particular, a full consideration of Donne would have to look at how he fits into the context of seventeenth-century literature and thinking. But an exploration of his achievement as a writer is not going to have much point unless it starts with the kind of detailed work on a number of his poems that I have suggested here. And what I think will always emerge from close work on his texts is this sense of Donne as a kind of juggler with words, only establishing a precarious hold on things that might fall apart at any moment.

## T. S. Eliot

The major idea that developed in my discussion of Donne was that difficult poetry not only offers us a very full sense of the disorder of experience but is also very tentative or precarious in the order it establishes, as if the artist is aware of the danger of imposing too simple a pattern upon experience. It takes great skill to write in this way, as the author must keep things open and not impose too rigid a control. Just as Donne makes tremendous use of the conceit as his central device for expressing both a sense of life's diversity and his activity as a poet, so other authors must all find their own original ways of conveying their distinctive views. We, as readers, are also, however, faced with a challenge, for when we are reading such major writers we must try to resist the temptation to reduce their works to a message, and instead try to remain alert to that wavering balance in their poems. These ideas, and a sense of how a different poet can find different techniques, should dominate in the following discussion of Eliot. However, rather than presuming too much in advance, I want to do as I have done throughout this book and try to build a picture of Eliot from the actual evidence of his poetry. The only difference is that on this occasion I am going to work from just one poem, *The Waste Land*, which is Eliot's major achievement, and many would say the most significant poem of the twentieth century. If you can understand *The Waste Land*, then you should not find it all that difficult to come to terms with other poems by Eliot. It is, unfortunately, too long to quote in its entirety here, but the short sections I work from should give you some sense of the poem as a whole.

1   *Look for a central opposition in the poem*

These are the opening lines of *The Waste Land*:

> April is the cruellest month, breeding
> Lilacs out of the dead land, mixing
> Memory and desire, stirring
> Dull roots with spring rain.
> Winter kept us warm, covering
> Earth in forgetful snow, feeding
> A little life with dried tubers.
> Summer surprised us, coming over the Starnbergersee
> With a shower of rain; we stopped in the colonnade,
> And went on in sunlight, into the Hofgarten,
> And drank coffee, and talked for an hour.
> Bin gar keine Russin, stamm' aus Litauen, echt deutsch.
> And when we were children, staying at the arch-duke's,
> My cousin's, he took me out on a sled,
> And I was frightened. He said, Marie,
> Marie, hold on tight. And down we went.
> In the mountains, there you feel free.
> I read, much of the night, and go south in the winter.

Any inexperienced reader of poetry encountering 'The Waste Land' for the first time is likely to find it incomprehensible. It is a long poem, divided into six sections, each of which has a fairly cryptic title such as 'The Burial of the Dead' or 'A Game of Chess'. Long poems are often narrative poems, where we can hang on to the story, but *The Waste Land* seems at the opposite remove from this, consisting instead of a disjointed sequence of verse paragraphs. The content of any one of these paragraphs, such as the opening lines above, is also likely to prove confusing because of the absence of an obvious thread running through it. When a poem is this bewildering, what we have to tell ourselves is that even the most unconventional poem must be dealing with those issues that have concerned all poets at all times, and that if we look at the opening lines we should be able to discover a familiar theme. In the case of *The Waste Land*, a look at just the two opening lines may enable us to make some progress:

> April is the cruellest month, breeding
> Lilacs out of the dead land . . . .

This might seem unpromising, but ask yourself some simple questions. For example, how do we usually think of April? I think it must be obvious that we regard it as the month of spring and renewal. Eliot, however, describes it in very different terms. It is a cruel month, and there is something chilling in the signs of growth as lilacs bloom out of 'the dead land'. Our normal associations of April do, however, serve to create an opposition. The poem is setting an idea of a life-giving, beneficial renewal in the natural order against a vision of a world which has become hard and cruel. The title sums up neatly one half of the tension: Eliot is contrasting a wasteland with the concept of growth and life. This, I would suggest, sets us up with a sense of a theme for the poem. Eliot is confronting a bleak and dispiriting world, but is likely to be searching for some significance, some meaning, some signs of order or promise within such an existence.

You might express your sense of the theme in different terms from those I have used. The vital point, however, is that you strive to capture and state the theme of the poem in brief and simple terms at the outset. Even with the most complicated poem, you need to express the central theme in a nutshell; if you can do this, you then have a firm foundation on which you can build the rest of your analysis. If, however, you fail to get hold of a theme at the outset, everything you say subsequently is likely to lack direction and purpose. Do try very hard, therefore, with any poem, to unlock it in this kind of decisive way, for that will enable you to explore the poem confidently.

2   *Begin to look at the details of the poem, trying to see how the poet brings his theme to life*

The tension in the poem is a very familiar one: in general terms we can say that an unhappy vision of the world is being set against a search for happiness. More specifically, we could say that Eliot is looking for genuine signs of spring and renewal in a cruel world. What we need to do now is look at how Eliot brings that theme to life: how he manages to create a picture of a disordered world and how he manages to suggest some concept of order. Eliot's technique might strike you as odd, but essentially we are looking for the kind of poetic features that I have described throughout this book. An analysis of these lines from the opening paragraph should make this clear:

Summer surprised us, coming over the Starnbergersee
With a shower of rain; we stopped in the colonnade,
And went on in sunlight, into the Hofgarten,
And drank coffee, and talked for an hour.
Bin gar keine Russin, stamm' aus Litauen, echt deutsch.

These lines are obviously hard to understand, yet they must be
working to establish the picture of the world that Eliot wants to
present to us. So far I have characterised this world as cruel and
bleak, but the images employed here fill out that initial impression.
As always, however, because they are images, rather than the poet
making a direct statement, every reader will respond to the words
in a different way and thus develop his or her own sense of the
characteristics of this world. What strikes me, for example, is that,
after the unconventional impression of April, the conjunction here
of summer and rain suggests that a traditional order has been lost,
and even the seasons are all awry. I also get a sense of a rootless
existence, of a wandering life on the continent, and the rapidity of
the shift from image to image suggests something nervous and
insubstantial about this existence. Your impressions, as I say,
might be different from mine, but can you see how the poet is using
simple techniques to create a sense of disorder, and in doing so
adds to our awareness of the problem he confronts? The line that
suddenly appears in a foreign language adds to this impression; we
do not need to look through the line and discover its meaning. We
should trust our initial response to the line, which disorients and
confuses us, and see that this works effectively to add to the
impression of an unstable, unsettled, nomadic existence. It is, of
course, a very negative sense of the world that is being created, yet
the very negative quality of the picture makes us reflect on a
traditional stability which Eliot must feel is missing in modern life.

What appears to be a difficult poem to understand is, I hope it
is becoming clear, not all that difficult to follow once we see that
fragmented and confusing images must work to present a fragmented
and confused sense of the world. Eliot's verse is fragmentary in
three ways: each verse paragraph seems to bear only an awkward
relationship to the preceding paragraph; on a line-by-line basis
there is often a disconcerting shift from idea to idea; and the
individual images are also fragmentary and disconcerting. If we
return again to trying to state the theme, we can talk about how
Eliot is searching for some sense of wholeness in a fragmented
world. We have already looked at how he establishes a fragmented

world, so now it might be a good idea to start searching for some suggestions of order and wholeness in the poem. As good a place as any to look is at the beginning of the second verse paragraph:

> What are the roots that clutch, what branches grow
> Out of this stony rubbish? Son of man,
> You cannot say, or guess, for you know only
> A heap of broken images, where the sun beats,
> And the dead tree gives no shelter, the cricket no relief . . . .

Images of disorder and waste are again much in evidence here: it has become a world of stony rubbish, where nothing grows. We confront a world of 'broken images', a world where everything has collapsed into bits and pieces. These images make Eliot's idea vivid, but each additional image adds to the idea, for it broadens our sense of something that has gone wrong in the order of things. The use of nature-images here, for example, extends the issue beyond social breakdown, which tended to be central in the first paragraph, and makes it a more general breakdwon in the whole order of existence. The result is very impressive, but the essential method is quite simple: Eliot uses images from all kinds of areas of experience to describe the issue so that we are presented with a very broad vision of life falling apart and dying.

What gives this vision real force, however, is the implicit sense that there must be some alternative. By referring to 'roots' and 'branches' Eliot points to what is missing, and what this amounts to is simply an idea of natural growth. There are other ways, though, in which the lines suggest a concept of order. The most basic one is the fact that these are lines of verse: the very fact of writing poetry sets a concept of pattern and meaning against a picture of the disorder of experience; the very structure of verse comments on a world where traditional structures seem to have been destroyed. Something like verse structure, however, affects meaning in a covert way. More obvious is the poet's use of imagery: in this instance, 'Son of man', a reference to Ezekiel, might also suggest 'Son of God' and, for me at least, the picture of this parched wasteland triggers off the idea of Christ in the wilderness. If this is at all credible, then the poem at this stage is hinting at the concept of a religious order in existence. In this way, then, the poem is setting images which substantiate and fill out a vision of a disordered world against images which hint at a concept of order.

3  *Look at another section of the poem, trying to see how the poem is progressing*

I seem above to have explained away all the problems; I seem to have suggested that Eliot writes in just the same way as any other writer. This is, however, not the case: every great writer has his own vision of the world which can only be expressed through his discovering fresh ways of writing. Let us, therefore, look at another section to pursue this idea:

> Madame Sosostris, famous clairvoyante,
> Had a bad cold, nevertheless
> Is known to be the wisest woman in Europe,
> With a wicked pack of cards.‑Here, said she,
> Is your card, the drowned Phoenician Sailor,
> (Those are pearls that were his eyes. Look!)....

The sudden, unexpected shift to this new character begins to define Eliot's originality. His poetry is more fragmentary than any poetry that had appeared before. The very piecemeal nature of his method seems appropriate for the twentieth century: he helps create the twentieth-century sense that we live in a jumbled, irrational, bizarre world where any sense of a larger meaning is missing. The particular images here also suggest a sordid quality to modern life, apparent in turning to fortune-tellers rather than trusting to any traditional sense of God. Yet the introduction of the Tarot cards maintains the tension of the poem, for it again raises the idea of the search for meaning and significance in experience.

What we can see in the way of technique, then, is that Eliot uses traditional methods, but innovates in the area of daring to offer a more fragmentary style which enables him to present a particularly disconcerting modern vision. Most of the techniques employed, however, are those that we should be familiar with from all poetry. I have mentioned, for example, how some images always work in the same way to create the same associations, and we can assume that *The Waste Land* will set light against dark in a traditional way. Let us look more particularly, however, at Eliot's use of images of dryness and wetness: the previous extract we examined had dry and stony images; in this extract, there is a reference to a drowned sailor. The poem seems to be using images of extremes of wetness and dryness: it is not presuming too much to guess that a positive value could be presented as just natural rainfall gently nurturing the land. The poem is, therefore, using the standard associations of traditional images to bring its theme to life and also add to the overall meaning of the poem.

It is much the same when Eliot writes of the 'pearls that were his eyes': he is exploiting the difference between seeing and blindness, these positive and negative associations adding to our sense of the central tension in the poem. But, if the use of imagery is to some extent conventional, what is also in evidence here is Eliot's innovative fragmentary method, for this line about pearls is a literary allusion, a snatch from another work that Eliot has incorporated into his own poem. If you have to study *The Waste Land* you will soon discover that it is full of such allusions. You will also need to develop a theory to explain their presence. Do not waste too much time looking up the references; what you really want to discover is the function they serve in the poem, how they contribute to its overall meaning. As fragments from literary works they very effectively suggest how the modern world has collapsed into fragments, yet also remind us how writers in the past did have some sense of wholeness, how they did manage to perceive a larger order in life. Again, then, Eliot has discovered a method that allows him to present an unique vision of the disorder of the modern world. At the same time, however, the allusions do keep before us the desire for a sense of wholeness: they remind us that in the past writers did seem to be able to make sense of the world in a coherent manner. In terms of form, *The Waste Land* lacks that traditional kind of coherence. It seems fragmentary and piecemeal. But it is not entirely like this: there is control, and a search for a pattern in evidence all the time. Any meaning in the poem is therefore created in the space between Eliot's sense of the fragmented complexity of life and his desire to see a pattern in life.

Rather than pursue this idea in general terms, however, let us see how it is evident in a further extract from the poem. These lines are from the middle section, 'The Fire Sermon':

'On Margate Sands.
I can connect
Nothing with nothing.
The broken fingernails of dirty hands.
My people humble people who expect
Nothing.'
       la la

To Carthage then I came

Burning burning burning burning
O Lord Thou pluckest me out
O Lord Thou pluckest

burning

This is another section that might seem baffling, but Eliot is speaking very directly at points here; nothing could be much more explicit than 'I can connect / Nothing with nothing.' It is a kind of low point in the poem where everything seems to have fragmented, and where Eliot seems to have broken down into silence and an inability to express himself. This is also evident in the primitive verse structure, with quite astonishingly short lines, as if no sort of more ambitious poetic structure can be put together. The poet's ability to speak almost disappears in 'la la'.

It would, in fact, be possible to stop at that point in an analysis of this extract. I have, after all, managed to capture an impression of how Eliot conveys the fragmented bleakness of existence. To my mind, however, such a reading reduces the effect of the poem, making too much of one half of its order/disorder opposition. If we stick with this passage we should be able to see that it has positive as well as negative implications. If we start with structure, I have suggested that the usual line discipline of poetry appears to be in ruins here, yet Eliot is still continuing to write poetry in lines, and this must tantalise us with some possibility of poetic order. The broken phrase 'la la' is double-edged in the same kind of way: it could represent speech falling apart, yet 'la la' can be read as a basic representation of song. It is as if, even in the midst of everything seeming futile, there is some movement towards harmony. What I am talking about here is the same kind of quality I drew attention to in Donne's poetry: the way in which the poet confronts the complexity of existence yet is also considering some precarious concept of order in existence, the way in which he confronts a world that possibly is without meaning yet always pursues the possibility of meaning. It is an ambivalent quality that is present all the time. A lesser poet might offer a more unrelenting picture of gloom or offer a glib solution, but here, as in all great poetry, there is a trembling instability between the facts of disorder and the dream of order. The difficulty for us as readers is that we are likely to make too much of either Eliot the pessimist or Eliot who seeks a Christian answer, and in so doing fail to do justice to the open, fluctuating quality of the poem.

The effect I am describing is apparent in Eliot's use of imagery in this passage. The concept of burning might seem entirely destructive, and when the word is repeated four times in a line Eliot seems to have yielded to a destructive force. Yet the very next line, 'O Lord Thou pluckest me out', confronts us with the suggestion that it might be a burning of purification and salvation. Certainly, when 'burning' appears on its own as the last line of this section, my impression is that it does carry positive as well as negative implications.

### 4    *Look at how the poem concludes*

This balance in the verse is wavering rather than poised and Eliot manages the whole time to acknowledge both life's complexity and the search for some simple pattern of truth in experience. This is particularly apparent as we move towards the end of *The Waste Land*:

> In this decayed hole among the mountains
> In the faint moonlight, the grass is singing
> Over the tumbled graves, above the chapel
> There is the empty chapel, only the wind's home.
> It has no windows, and the door swings,
> Dry bones can harm no one.
> Only a cock stood on the rooftree
> Co co rico co co rico
> In a flash of lightning. Then a damp gust
> Bringing rain

I have said before that the central tension of a poem is resolved in some way at the end of the poem, and here there is a considerable relief in tension as the rain actually comes. But any relief is suggested rather than stated: the image of a chapel, for example, carries certain implications, but any suggestion of harmony is implicit rather than explicit. We search for meaning in what appear to us to be significant images. The result is that right through to the end there is a trembling, precarious balance as the poem both confronts the world and tantalises us with concepts of meaning and wholeness.

5 *Sum up your sense of the poem as a whole, and your sense of the writer so far*

There are many other ways in which *The Waste Land* needs to be explored, but I hope I have managed to get across here how it is possible to start making sense of even the most puzzling modern poem. The kind of thinking that is at the heart of *The Waste Land* informs a great deal of modern poetry, for all twentieth-century writers find themselves confronted by a similar dilemma: this is that they live in a complex world where any sense of a traditional order, such as faith in God, has virtually disappeared. They will therefore, like Eliot, be particularly concerned to confront and present a vision of a complex world, and, equally, ask basic questions about whether there is a meaning and significance in experience. But the finest, such as Eliot, are likely to maintain a wavering tension between both sides of the case, neither giving way to a sense of despair nor opting for glib consolation in too-simple answers.

## William Wordsworth

What I have been praising in Donne and Eliot is an unresolved quality in their verse whereby they let us feel both the complexity of life and the desire to see a meaning in life. At first sight Wordsworth seems a different kind of writer, for he appears to have a philosophy, a clearly defined set of convictions that he presents in his poetry. He seems to present us with a very confident sense of an order that he can perceive in experience. Rather than explain these views here, however, let us turn to one of Wordsworth's poems and follow our usual procedure of trying to build a picture of the writer from his actual words. The poem I start with is **'Expostulation and Reply'**:

'Why, William, on that old grey stone,
Thus for the length of half a day,
Why, William, sit you thus alone,
And dream your time away?

'Where are your books? – that light bequeathed
To Beings else forlorn and blind!

Up! up! and drink the spirit breathed
From dead men to their kind.

'You look round on your Mother Earth,
As if she for no purpose bore you;
As if you were her first-born birth,
And none had lived before you!'

One morning thus, by Esthwaite lake,
When life was sweet, I knew not why,
To me my good friend Matthew spake,
And thus I made reply:

'The eye – it cannot choose but see;
We cannot bid the ear be still;
Our bodies feel, where'er they be,
Against or with our will.

'Nor less I deem that there are Powers
Which of themselves our minds impress:
That we can feed this mind of ours
In a wise passiveness.

'Think you, 'mid all this mighty sum
Of things for ever speaking,
That nothing of itself will come;
But we must still be seeking?

'– Then ask not wherefore, here, alone,
Conversing as I may,
I sit upon this old grey stone,
And dream my time away.'

1   *Look for a central opposition in the poem*

In the first two stanzas of the poem, a friend asks Wordsworth why
he spends so much time just sitting on an old grey stone; he urges
Wordsworth to employ his time more usefully. He urges him to
read, for in books the wisdom of the past is handed down to us.
The opposition, then, is between the apparently idle Wordsworth
and his energetic friend. If we try to establish a theme here, we

might notice that the friend talks of the 'light bequeathed' from books, a light than can illuminate darkness. What we might suspect, however, even this early in the poem, is that Wordsworth, while apparently idling his time away, senses a far truer light. It seems reasonable, even this early, to surmise that he is in possession of some kind of inner peace which can be set against the hurly-burly of the world.

2  *Begin to look at the details of the poem, trying to see how the poet brings his theme to life*

We can now move forward to a consideration of the straightforward ways in which imagery and verse structure begin to give force to Wordsworth's theme. I am particularly struck by the difference between the third and fourth stanzas:

'You look round on your Mother Earth,
As if she for no purpose bore you;
As if you were her first-born birth,
And none had lived before you!'

One morning thus, by Esthwaite lake,
When life was sweet, I knew not why,
To me my good friend Matthew spoke,
And thus I made reply . . . .

Which of these two stanzas do you find more attractive? My own preference is for the second, because it seems so simple and natural. The sentence structure is uncomplicated, and everything is very concrete. There is the substantiality of 'by Esthwaite lake', and the direct statement of 'When life was sweet'. By comparison, the words of the friend seem abstract and pompous. The friend seems to spend too much time thinking, whereas Wordsworth does not seem to need to think: he just accepts the sweetness of life, telling us, 'I knew not why'.

My impression of the poem so far is that it is simple yet effective. I also feel I can now say quite a lot about Wordsworth's ideas. He seems to offer a sense of harmony which is simple and non-intellectual, and this seems to be characterised in particular by a close harmony between man and nature. If you have been studying Wordsworth, that view of him might well seem familiar; you may even have been told that this was what Wordsworth believed in before you looked at his verse. What I hope I have shown here, however, is how quickly you can establish for yourself a clear sense of Wordsworth's positives from the evidence of the verse itself.

3   *Look at another section of the poem, trying to see how the poem is progressing*

Compared to the poems of Donne and Eliot that we have looked at, Wordsworth's poem seems very simple indeed. There is a neat tension in evidence, in which the positive, ordered view is very clear-cut. Things might, however, get more complicated as the poem continues, particularly as Wordsworth expands upon his position:

'The eye – it cannot choose but see;
We cannot bid the ear be still;
Our bodies feel, where'er they be
Against or with our will.

'Nor less I deem that there are Powers
Which of themselves our minds impress:
That we can feed this mind of ours
In a wise passiveness.

The language of the poem becomes more elaborate as Wordsworth offers a more developed impression of the harmony he senses in life. The essential techniques for suggesting this feeling are, however, simple. There is a relaxed, untroubled movement to these sentences which suggests a state of peace. In the first of these stanzas, it is evident that the human body becomes an element in a larger controlling order; in the second this order seems to be connected with some kind of spiritual force, as Wordsworth writes, 'I deem that there are Powers'. We receive a sense of a harmonious relationship between man, nature and the universe. The slightly inflated language, apparent in a word such as 'deem', invests the whole experience with a sense of importance.

4   *Look at how the poem concludes*

The poem started with a tension, the tension of a challenge as Wordsworth's friend questioned him. By the end, the tension has gone; Wordsworth has the answer:

'– Then ask not wherefore, here, alone.
Conversing as I may,
I sit upon this old grey stone,
And dream my time away.'

The images of the author himself and the old grey stone seem to sum up much of what the poem is about. He is close to an object in nature, but, more than that, it is as if there is some real sense of a larger order in the universe. The central stanzas of the poem have developed this idea, with the result that, when we return to the stone and the poet dreaming at the end, we feel that there is a weight of meaning implicit in these simple images.

5   *Sum up your sense of the poem as a whole, and your sense of the writer so far*

This is, to my mind, a very effective poem because of the economy and force with which Wordsworth presents his confident sense of an order that he can perceive in experience. As likeable as the poem is, however, I am sure that you can see that it is a simple poem compared to the other poems we have looked at in this chapter. Indeed, it can help us define that essential quality of impressive difficult poetry. In this poem the tension is simple and kept simple, with a very confident ordered view of the word being developed. A difficult poem would be likely to present us with a much fuller impression of the complexity of experience, and present a much more tentative suggestion of order. This poem is confident rather than tentative or self-questioning.

Perhaps Wordsworth is always like this. As I have said, he tends to be regarded as a poet with a philosophy. The only way to develop our impression of Wordsworth, however, is to keep on looking at his poems, so I shall now turn to **'Resolution and Independence'**. It is a longer poem than 'Expostulation and Reply', rather too long, unfortunately, to reproduce here in full, but the very fact of its length suggests that Wordsworth might use the space to develop and explore more complex issues than we have seen so far. We can -start with the opening stanza:

There was a roaring in the wind all night;
The rain came heavily and fell in floods;
But now the sun is rising calm and bright;
The birds are singing in the distant woods;
Over his own sweet voice the stock-dove broods;
The jay makes answer as the magpie chatters;
And all the air is fill'd with pleasant noise of waters.

1   *Look for a central opposition in the poem*

The poem starts with a description of the previous night's storm, but this soon gives way to feelings of happiness associated with the beauty of the day. A sense of disorder is inherent in the images of stormy weather and flooding. Set against this are images of pleasant weather. More seems to be suggested, however, than just a notion of pleasant weather; a strong sense of an idea of order in the natural world comes across. I am particularly struck by the line 'The jay makes answer as the magpie chatters': the birds seem to be conducting a conversation, and this seems to suggest that the separate parts of the natural world are not separate but all part of some larger pattern. It is, therefore, a harmonious vision of the world. This is also suggested by the attractive water image, the 'pleasant noise of waters', which can be set against the fury of the night's floods.

2   *Begin to look at the details of the poem, trying to see how the poet brings his theme to life*

The poem is already suggesting something of that sense of harmony in existence that we experienced in 'Expostulation and Reply'; the complication, however, is the previous night's storm. The poem has acknowledged a darker, more uncontrollable side of nature which cannot be swept aside just because a new day is dawning. And, indeed, as the poem goes on, Wordsworth describes how feelings of dejection can suddenly undercut feelings of joy:

To me that morning did it happen so;
And fears, and fancies, thick upon me came;
Dim sadness, and blind thoughts I knew not nor could name.

These lines strike me as more interesting than those of 'Expostulation and Reply' just because Wordsworth seems much more ready to face up to the dark and disordered side of experience. Dark, in fact, seems the appropriate word, for the images used to describe his feelings are 'dim' and 'blind'; the problem is that the dark will not go away. There is always the nagging disorder of experience. We can expect that the poem will have to develop a more complex vision of order than in 'Expostulation and Reply', for if Wordsworth is going to produce a containing, ordered vision it will have to cope with the complex and dark feelings expressed here.

3    *Look at another section of the poem, trying to see how the poem is progressing*

The main thing that happens in the course of the poem is that the poet encounters an old man:

> As a huge stone is sometimes seen to lie
> Couched on the bald top of an eminence;
> Wonder to all who do the same espy
> By what means it could thither come, and whence;
> So that it seems a thing endued with sense:
> Like a sea-beast crawl'd forth, that on a shelf
> Of rock or sand reposeth, there to sun itself;
>
> Such seem'd this Man, not all alive nor dead,
> Nor all asleep – in his extreme old age:
> His body was bent double, feet and head
> Coming together in life's pilgrimage;
> As if some dire constraint of pain, or rage
> Of sickness felt by him in times long past,
> A more than human weight upon his frame had cast.

This old man is introduced, but his relevance to the issues we have discussed so far is at first hard to see. The reason for this is that, in these stanzas at least, Wordsworth does not explain the old man's role but merely describes him. It is, however, not just a straightforward visual description. A variety of images are employed, such as the description of the old man in relation to 'a huge stone'. It is images such as these that begin to create meaning and significance, although, as everything is being suggested rather than stated, what that significance is remains uncertain for a while.

At this point, in fact, I decided to read on in the poem to see whether Wordsworth does offer us a direct explanation of the old man's function; some stanzas later, I came across this:

And the whole body of the Man did seem
Like one whom I had met with in a dream;
Or like a man from some far region sent,
To give me human strength, by apt admonishment.

Wordsworth makes a very direct statement here: the old man is such a symbol of endurance that he stands as a rebuke to the poet, who has been making too much of his own feelings of despondency. We seem to be back with the impression of Wordsworth as essentially a simple poet; the poem might be powerful, but its essential message seems straightforward. I wonder, however, whether things are as clear-cut as this; I am trying here to explore the feeling I have at the end of 'Resolution and Independence' that I have read a poem that is not comforting but disturbing. The materials of the poem will not seem to submit themselves to the neat, rather moral message that Wordsworth provides in the few lines quoted above. What I am talking about should already be apparent in the disparity between the comment of Wordsworth's and what I described as a rather puzzling impression of the old man that comes across in the two stanzas quoted earlier. There, I suggested, the images suggest a sense of the old man, but the very fact that Wordsworth employs images means that what is being suggested about him is not precise and moral. There now seems a gap between that complex and puzzling impression of the old man and the moral lesson that Wordsworth draws from his character. What I am suggesting is that the old man is a rather strange figure, and that Wordsworth seems to rush in rather too quickly to impose a meaning upon him and those stranger aspects of experience he suggests.

The fact that there is something strange and inexplicable about the old man is most evident when Wordsworth describes him as like a 'sea-beast'. This is a disturbing image. It seems to suggest the whole darker, concealed, furtive side of experience; in this respect it can be linked with the previous night's storm. And, just as a pleasant day cannot eliminate a memory of the night, so Wordsworth's readiness to find encouragement from the man's example cannot eliminate our sense that he is a disturbing and mysterious figure. It is as if there is a gap between the reality of the man and the significance that Wordsworth wishes to impose upon him; this is made dramatically clear when Wordsworth describes the old man speaking:

> The old Man still stood talking by my side;
> But now his voice to me was like a stream
> Scarce heard; nor word from word could I divide . . . .

Can you see how the poet does not actually listen to the old man? Wordsworth imposes a significance upon him, but that meaning is of Wordsworth's own making and does not cope with all the disturbing impressions he has created of the man.

### 4   *Look at how the poem concludes*

What I have described might be felt to be a shortcoming in the poem. We might seem to have uncovered Wordsworth's determination to turn the man into a poetic symbol. My own feeling, however, is that this uneasiness in the text makes this a more powerful poem. One of the weaknesses of poor poetry is that it does impose too neat and glib an order upon experience. This poem, by contrast, offers us the consoling force of the poet finding a meaning in experience, but leaves room for self-doubt as Wordsworth includes a sense of the old man which is at odds with the pattern-making impulse of the poem. Is this deliberate? I do not know. All I know is that the poem contains disturbing, suggestive images which do not tally with any neat moral meaning that Wordsworth might discover in experience. As such, Wordsworth is managing to suggest, as all great poets do, both the complexity of experience and our need to order experience, but also maintaining a wavering balance between the two, so that we are constantly aware of both the disordered and orderly elements in the poem. We can, in fact, express this in terms of the opening images of the poem: there is an ever-present tension between the clear light of day and the disturbing night.

At the end of 'Resolution and Independence', however, it is the positive sense that seems to dominate:

> And soon with this he other matter blended,
> Cheerfully uttered, with demeanour kind,

But stately in the main; and, when he ended,
I could have laugh'd myself to scorn to find
In that decrepit Man so firm a mind.
'God,' said I, 'be my help and stay secure;
I'll think of the Leech-gatherer on the lonely moor!'

This reiterates the idea of the old man as a rebuke to the poet, who should feel corrected by the forbearance and fortitude of the old man. And part of me wants to accept that ordered conclusion. But I do not feel entirely comfortable at the end of the poem: my sense of the dark night and the mysterious, disquieting qualities of the old man will not quite gel with the air of peace established here.

5   *Sum up your sense of the poem as a whole, and your sense of the writer so far*

There is then, for me at least, a sense here, as there is in so much great poetry, of the gap between the untidy reality of existence and the patterns that the artist imposes upon, or finds in, experience. The attraction of the poem is the very unstable nature of this tension, so that simultaneously we can feel the complexity of experience and the artist's desire to resolve that complexity. It is a gap between poetic rhetoric and prosaic reality, but the poetic rhetoric is important for we cannot just accept a dark or baffling world, we need to struggle to explain it.

It might still be felt, however, that this view in some ways lessens the importance of Wordsworth. For many people, Wordsworth's 'natural philosophy' has been a source of inspiration and strength. Can it really be dismissed, as I appear to be dismissing it here, as something that is not only faulty but also something that Wordsworth knows is faulty, and so questions and undermines in his own works? In order to explore this issue further, let us turn more directly to the question of how we respond to Wordsworth's vision of the world, as reflected in one of his very finest poems, **'Tintern Abbey'**. It is another long poem, but the lines quoted here should convey something of the sense and strength of it.

1   *Look for a central opposition in the poem*

'Tintern Abbey' starts with Wordsworth describing a remembered
landscape:

>                         Once again
> Do I behold these steep and lofty cliffs,
> Which on a wild secluded scene impress
> Thoughts of more deep seclusion; and connect
> The landscape with the quiet of the sky.
> The day is come when I again repose
> Here, under this dark sycamore, and view
> These plots of cottage-ground, these orchard-tufts,
> Which, at this season, with their unripe fruits,
> Are clad in one green hue, and lose themselves
> Among the woods and copses, nor disturb
> The wild green landscape. Once again I see
> These hedge-rows – hardly hedge-rows, little lines
> Of sportive wood run wild . . . .

This might appear to be just a description of the landscape, but the
poem must be announcing a theme even this early. What I would
suggest, from the idealised nature of the view here, is that
Wordsworth is providing an initial positive sense of the world and
that darker notes will appear as the poem continues. If we look
more closely at this picture of the landscape, however, we should
spot some interesting points. We have already seen above how
Wordsworth frequently writes of an order and harmony that he
perceives in the natural world. It is my impression that a strong
sense of that harmony and order is being created here. Look at how
everything interrelates in this picture; it all seems to fit together like
a jigsaw. Consider the lines: 'hedge-rows – hardly hedge-rows, little
lines / Of sportive wood run wild'. The force of this is that it makes
man's world, the cultivated hedgerows, and a wilder world of
nature, the wood, merge indistinguishably. The effect of such lines
is that they announce an order and harmony that Wordsworth can
perceive in the whole of existence.

He goes on to talk about this more extensively in the second
paragraph of the poem:

> While with an eye made quiet by the power
> Of harmony, and the deep power of joy,
> We see into the life of things.

Here we can see how Wordsworth's eye has been subdued by this greater power of harmony. In addition, the language has become more inflated, so that we feel a kind of awe at the inspiring order that Wordsworth perceives, an order that includes mankind.

2   *Begin to look at the details of the poem, trying to see how the poet brings his theme to life*

So far we have a sense of the world and an order that Wordsworth perceives in the world. The next paragraph begins with Wordsworth talking about this belief of his:

> If this
> Be but a vain belief, yet, oh! how oft,
> In darkness, and amid the many shapes
> Of joyless daylight; when the fretful stir
> Unprofitable, and the fever of the world,
> Have hung upon the beatings of my heart,
> How oft, in spirit, have I turned to thee,
> O sylvan Wye!

This strikes me as tentative. The confidence of the previous paragraph has gone as the light of illumination that shines there gives way to darkness. Look, for example, at the long, complicated sentence that stresses all the disorder of the world. It is only at the end of that sentence that Wordsworth returns to the fact that he at least has found comfort in nature; but at this stage it begins to seem like an acknowledgement that there is a gap between prosaic reality and the inspiring poetic rhetoric that can transform reality.

3   *Look at another section of the poem, trying to see how the poem is progressing*

An open and tentative structure is developing in the poem as Wordsworth begins to examine the characteristics of the order that he finds in or imposes upon reality. As the poem continues, he writes of how, as a youth, he could enjoy nature without needing to find any larger significance within the natural world. He then returns to his current state of mind:

                        That time is past,
And all its aching joys are now no more,
And all its dizzy raptures. Not for this
Faint I, nor mourn nor murmur; other gifts
Have followed, for such loss, I would believe,
Abundant recompense. For I have learned
To look on nature, not as in the hour
Of thoughtless youth, but hearing oftentimes
The still, sad music of humanity . . . .

The poem might have become tentative at times, but there seems
no room for doubt here as Wordsworth writes about his possession
of something valuable that makes life meaningful and worthwhile.
Yet I am not totally convinced; the poem has struck too many
worrying notes before this. The result, for me, is that there seems
something just a little too artificial and consoling about the sense of
order and significance that Wordsworth establishes here. The
tension is apparent in the lines themselves: boyhood was immediate
and physical, and is described in physical terms such as 'aching
joys' and 'dizzy raptures'. The new feeling he has discovered is
intellectual and expressed in abstract terms, such as 'The still, sad
music of humanity': this is a very attractive line, but to my mind
has just the merest hint of contrivance and exaggeration. I am not,
of course, dismissing outright Wordsworth's positive feelings: they
must come across to us from the poem in a powerful way. But what
I am saying is that the order he establishes in the poem is
precarious, that we are still conscious of the darker side of life, of all
those feelings and experiences that can undermine the poet's
achieved order. What is in evidence again, then, is that wavering
balance of a great poem, whereby we are simultaneously aware of
both the complexity of reality and the author finding a significant
pattern in experience. But neither side dominates. As readers we
are struck by both the ordered shape of the poem and the fact that
the ordered shape has a kind of provisional quality to it, as if it
could crumble at any moment.

4   *Look at how the poem concludes*

At the end of 'Tintern Abbey', Wordsworth considers how he
might feel if he had not been brought up and educated in the way
he has been:

> Nor, perchance,
> If I were not thus taught, should I the more
> Suffer my genial spirits to decay:
> For thou art with me, here, upon the banks
> Of this fair river; thou, my dearest friend,
> My dear, dear friend, and in thy voice I catch
> The language of my former heart, and read
> My former pleasures in the shooting lights
> Of thy wild eyes.

The 'friend' he is talking to is his sister. His examination of how he would feel if the circumstances of his life had been different relates in an interesting way to everything he has said so far. It provides a further acknowledgement that this is a very personal order that he perceives in experience, and therefore that its general relevance and value might be open to question. It might be a false kind of comfort that he has devised for himself. Can you see how this maintains a kind of sceptical self-questioning that has been in evidence throughout the poem? There is tremendous power in Wordsworth's evocation of the harmony he can see in experience; there is something very inspiring about the kind of relationship between man, nature and the universe that he celebrates. And the language of his poems is often at the most exciting at those points where he combines and fuses images from these three areas of experience. But what I am suggesting is that the verse is more complex than this, that he questions and explores the nature of the harmony he establishes. And the ways in which he does this have to be the ways that all poets employ to make their poems come to life. First of all there is the structure of the poem: ordered lines will suggest the order that Wordsworth sees, but as a whole the poem is diffuse and rambling, and this provides us with a constant sense of the untidy nature of reality, that the shape of reality and the shape of the poet's vision are likely to be at odds. The other way Wordsworth creates a complex sense of life's complexity is through his use of imagery: in 'Resolution and Independence' the image of the old man was sufficiently uncomfortable and disquieting to challenge and undermine the poetic significance that Wordsworth wished to impose upon him. To my mind, it is much the same in this poem: the images provide us with a sufficiently full sense of the more diverse and dark sides of experience to challenge and partly undermine the order that Wordsworth creates within the poem.

5  *Sum up your sense of the poem as a whole, and your sense of the writer*
   *so far*

It might still seem that I am dismissing the importance of
Wordsworth's vision, as if I am trying to find faults in his poems.
This, however, is not the case. To my mind a poem becomes more
powerful when the poet both establishes his vision and at the same
time admits the shortcomings of that vision. Such a poem, whilst
revealing our shared desire to make sense of the world, also
acknowledges the complexity of the world.

## Samuel Taylor Coleridge

Coleridge, a close friend of Wordsworth's, might seem to be the
exact opposite of Wordsworth as a poet. Wordsworth (although I
hope I have shown he is not a simple writer) can seem a
straightforward, moral poet concerned to make a point. Coleridge
is at the opposite extreme from straightforwardness. He is likely to
strike the reader as a poet whose works are always obscure, and in
whose poems any kind of meaning seems almost impossible to be
sure about. This should become apparent as we look at one of his
most famous poems, '**Kubla Khan**':

> In Xanadu did Kubla Khan
> A stately pleasure-dome decree:
> Where Alph, the sacred river, ran
> Through caverns measureless to man
>     Down to a sunless sea.
> So twice five miles of fertile ground
> With walls and towers were girdled round:
> And there were gardens bright with sinous rills
> Where blossomed many an incense-bearing tree;
> And here were forests ancient as the hills,
> Enfolding sunny spots of greenery.
>
> But oh! that deep romantic chasm which slanted
> Down the green hill athwart a cedarn cover!
> A savage place! as holy and enchanted
> As e'er beneath a waning moon was haunted
> By woman wailing for her demon-lover!

And from this chasm, with ceaseless turmoil seething,
As if this earth in fast thick pants was breathing,
A mighty fountain momently was forced:
Amid whose swift half-intermitted burst
Huge fragments vaulted like rebounding hail,
Or chaffy grain beneath the thresher's flail:
And 'mid these dancing rocks at once and ever
It flung up momently the sacred river.
Five miles meandering with a mazy motion
Through wood and dale the sacred river ran,
Then reached the caverns measureless to man,
And sank in tumult to a lifeless ocean:
And 'mid this tumult Kubla heard from afar
Ancestral voices prophesying war!

   The shadow of the dome of pleasure
   Floated midway on the waves;
   Where was heard the mingled measure
   From the fountain and the caves.
It was a miracle of rare device,
A sunny pleasure-dome with caves of ice!

   A damsel with a dulcimer
   In a vision once I saw:
   It was an Abyssinian maid,
   And on her dulcimer she played,
   Singing of Mount Abora.
   Could I revive within me,
   Her symphony and song,
   To such a deep delight 'twould win me,
That with music loud and long,
I would build that dome in air,
That sunny dome! those caves of ice!
And all who heard should see them there.
And all should cry, Beware! Beware!
His flashing eyes, his floating hair!
Weave a circle round him thrice,
And close your eyes with holy dread,
For he on honey-dew hath fed,
And drunk the milk of Paradise.

1   *Look for a central opposition in the poem*

This is a fascinating poem, presenting the most extraordinary pictures, but what is it about? Let us take a closer look at the first five lines:

In Xanadu did Kubla Khan
A stately pleasure-dome decree:
Where Alph, the sacred river, ran
Through caverns measureless to man
Down to a sunless sea.

I can see an opposition here, between the architectural image of the dome that Kubla Khan builds and the wildness of the 'caverns measureless to man', but what significance can be read into this opposition? It is hard to say with any confidence, because Coleridge is employing symbols. A symbol, such as the 'pleasure-dome', seems full of meaning, but the poet does not offer us a firm sense of its significance. A symbol might seem to be just the same as an image, but an image is either something from normal experience that the writer includes in the poem or a linking of one area of experience with another area of experience. The point about an image is that either it helps define experiences or else there is a clear context of association for it to work in, but with a symbol we are given less guidance and obliged to infer more. If, for example, a poet writes 'My love is like a red, red rose', there is the concrete image of his lover and the figurative association with a rose; to a large extent the terms are being defined. When Coleridge offers us the symbol of the 'pleasure-dome', however, there are no real clues as to what is being implied; there is no explanatory framework within the poem.

It is, therefore, not surprising that symbolism can mislead students. It can lead to the idea that there are hidden meanings in poetry, and this in turn can lead to over-ingenuity in inventing a meaning. Or, as sometimes happens in the case of Coleridge, it can make the reader feel that everything is so mysterious that we cannot pin down a meaning for the poem. You might well come across the information that 'Kubla Khan' was written under the influence of drugs, or that the poem features cryptic symbols dredged up from Coleridge's unconscious mind which have no relation to the real world or rational thought. To regard the poem as just a drug-induced vision is, however, to belittle it as eccentric.

Like any great poem it must be dealing with the problems that concern all men at all times.

This really provides us with our major clue for interpreting the poem, including the symbols. We know that writers often confront the seeming disorder of experience and try to discover or create some sense of order. If we look at the opening of 'Kubla Khan', the idea of 'measureless' caverns does seem to suggest one side of that tension, the idea of an infinite, unmappable world. As against this, the building of the pleasure-dome suggests the creation of order over chaos. I must add, however, that this is purely a speculative reading; it is a way of making sense of the material which is in line with our standard expectations of poetry. Indeed, the very presence of the symbols points again to the kind of difficulty there is in understanding great poetry that I have written about throughout this chapter; as the symbols do not have a precise meaning, there is, throughout the poem, a sense of a complex and mysterious world. Any order established is likely to be very precarious or artificial.

2   *Begin to look at the details of the poem, trying to see how the poet brings his theme to life*

Coleridge continues by describing the gardens and then the forests of Xanadu.

> A savage place! as holy and enchanted
> As e'er beneath a waning moon was haunted
> By woman wailing for her demon-lover!
> And from this chasm, with ceaseless turmoil seething,
> As if this earth in fast thick pants were breathing,
> A mighty fountain momently was forced . . . .

The lines are again hard to understand both because the pictures are strange and because there is no explanation. What comes across however, with the references to savagery, a woman wailing, and turmoil, is a sense of wild instincts that are hidden below the surface. But because more is being suggested than is ever stated or explained, different responses may strike you. It seems to me, for example, that a number of the words have sexual implications; when they are combined they offer a sense of a dark and uncontrollable force. There is, however, no authorisation for this reading; what I am doing is pinning down a meaning on symbols.

It is, however, wrong to pin down too precise a meaning, for an essential part of the force of symbols is that they are vague and suggest the strange and unknown; they enact the idea of the mystery of experience, and consequently make us feel the difficulty of imposing order upon chaos. I can say, though, that the poem is offering a powerful, yet non-specific, sense of disorderly, wild, natural forces in experience. Yet, as powerful as these impressions are, the poem must do more than just offer chaotic and disturbing impressions; there must be some kind of attempt to confront the chaos, just as Kubla Khan built his pleasure-dome.

3   *Look at another section of the poem, trying to see how the poem is progressing*

There are some quite alarming changes of direction in the poem; most notably when Coleridge shifts to this picture of a young woman:

> A damsel with a dulcimer
> In a vision once I saw;
> It was an Abyssinian maid,
> And on her dulcimer she played,
> Singing of Mount Abora.
> Could I revive within me
> Her symphony and song,
> To such a deep delight 'twould win me,
> That with music loud and long
> I would build that dome in air . . . .

I shall start by trying to pin down some kind of meaning here. There is something in the notion of the girl playing a tune on the dulcimer that suggests an idea of harmony; then Coleridge goes on to suggest that if he could revive that memory he could build a dome. These are orderly images; Coleridge seems to be writing about his desire to impose a musical or poetic pattern upon the world. Yet again, then, we see an artist striving to order experience. The actual pictures presented in these lines do, however, undercut or seem to make impossible that desire to create a precarious hold on the world. The idea of the damsel, and particularly such details as her dulcimer and the fact that she is Abyssinian, is so exotic that it works against the attempt to interpret and understand the world. Yet part of the excitement in the poem is provided by Coleridge feeling that he can just about hold together a vision of life that takes account of all its complexity.

### 4   *Look at how the poem concludes*

The poem ends by returning again to the idea of the poet:

> And all who heard should see them there,
> And all should cry, Beware! Beware!
> His flashing eyes, his floating hair!
> Weave a circle round him thrice,
> And close your eyes with holy dread,
> For he on honey-dew hath fed,
> And drunk the milk of Paradise.

This is a vision of the poet who has built a dome; he is so powerful that he is worshipped. A sense of order, and the order of art, might therefore seem to dominate at the end of the poem, yet the picture created again undercuts the sense of an achieved significance. It is as simple as the fact that the poet seems strange, unnatural and disturbing: a sense of the mysterious again conflicts with the desire to interpret experience.

### 5   *Sum up your sense of the poem as a whole, and your sense of the writer so far*

You might feel that it is still far from clear what 'Kubla Khan' is actually about. The reading I have produced might make it appear an esoteric poem about the art of poetry. But it is dealing with the universal issues of the complexity of existence and our need to try to understand experience. What makes the poem so exciting is the way in which it deploys its symbols and the way in which it uses poetic structure. The symbols suggest a dark and mysterious world: they seem to plunge into a concealed world, including the world of the unconscious mind. It is all a step further on from the use of imagery we have been examining so far: imagery can suggest the diffuseness and diversity of experience, but it all seems within the sphere of a knowable world. Symbolism suggests the unfathomable, the unmappable, and the unconscious. Yet at times Coleridge seems to be getting possession of that world, as if his poetic structure can contain and explain it. This is most evident when the poem becomes most incantatory or musical, as if Coleridge were finding an answer in the shape and sound and movement of poetry. Yet, as in all great poetry, that hold is precarious, and the chaos of experience keeps on flooding back in.

'Kubla Khan', we can conclude, is a strange poem, but we must never lose sight of the fact that what helps make it an important poem is that it deals with the issues that all poets deal with, and confronts the problems that all humanity confronts. Much the same judgement should also apply to Coleridge's other oustandingly famous poem **'The Ancient Mariner'**. It is a very long poem, so I cannot quote all of it here. I shall also keep my analysis of it as brief as possible, since what I want to do in the closing pages of this chapter is try to highlight in the simplest form possible the ideas that I have developed in it.

1    *Look for a central opposition in the poem*

The poem starts with an aged mariner stopping a wedding-guest:

It is an ancient Mariner
And he stoppeth one of three.
'By thy long grey beard and glittering eye,
Now wherefore stopp'st thou me?

The Bridegroom's doors are opened wide,
And I am next of kin;
The guests are met, the feast is set:
Mayst hear the merry din.'

He holds him with his skinny hand,
'There was a ship,' quoth he.
'Hold off! unhand me, grey-beard loon!'
Eftsoons his hand dropt he.

We need to establish an opposition. A wedding is obviously a time of happiness and rejoicing. In an indirect way, the mention of the wedding makes us consider the whole concept of marriage, which is the central social institution, the secure framework within which most people choose to live. Yet on the occasion of this wedding the guest is approached by a mysterious figure. It seems fair to say, therefore, that the theme of the poem promises to be the intrusion of the strange and disturbing into everyday life.

2   *Begin to look at the details of the poem, trying to see how the poet, brings his theme to life*

What happens in 'The Ancient Mariner' is that the mariner tells the tale of how he shot an albatross, and the strange events that ensued. An appropriate passage to look at now is a section that appears just after the albatross has been shot, when things are beginning to go wrong:

> The very deep did rot: O Christ!
> That ever this should be!
> Yea, slimy things did crawl with legs
> Upon the slimy sea.
>
> About, about, in reel and rout
> The death-fires danced at night;
> The water, like a witch's oils,
> Burnt green, and blue and white.
>
> And some in dreams assurèd were
> Of the spirit that plagued us so;
> Nine fathom deep he had followed us
> From the land of mist and snow.

I want to keep my comments on this poem very brief, so will limit myself to mentioning the sense of something grim and macabre that has been released. It is as if the mariner, by his act of destruction, has broken all the rules of behaviour with the result that, with the veneer of civilisation gone, disturbing forces become evident. The principal method of bringing this to life in the poem is the use of appropriately disturbing impressions of strange forces.

3   *Look at another section of the poem, trying to see how the poem is progressing*

> I looked to heaven, and tried to pray;
> But or ever a prayer had gusht,
> A wicked whisper came, and made
> My heart as dry as dust.

I closed my lids, and kept them close,
And the balls like pulses beat;
For the sky and the sea, and the sea and the sky
Lay like a load on my weary eye,
And the dead were at my feet.

One unusual feature of 'The Ancient Mariner' is that Coleridge
provides notes in the margin. If you bother to read these notes you will
see that they offer a moral meaning to the poem, centring on the need
to respect all forms of life. These two stanzas I have just quoted seem
to endorse that sense of the poem, for they start with the concepts of
faith and prayer and God's order.

This returns us, however, to the issue we have been looking at
throughout this chapter, the issue of what is being said in a difficult
poem. It would be possible to argue that the purpose of 'The
Ancient Mariner' is moral; we could put together a neat and
coherent response along these lines, using stanzas such as these to
substantiate our case. Here, for example, there is a positive idea of
turning to God and putting one's faith in God. The problem with
such a coherent reading of the poem, however, is that it seems to
sweep out of existence all those disturbing elements we have
already seen in the earlier stanzas quoted. They offer us a strong
sense of the dark mysteries of existence; the simple concept of
Christian prayer does not, in the overall context of this poem,
outweigh and banish those disturbing forces. As in 'Kubla Khan',
Coleridge uses symbols: the way in which he uses the sea, the sun
and all the surrounding references creates a sense of unfathomable
mysteries.

4   *Look at how the poem concludes*

As we might expect, an ordered note dominates at the end of the
poem:

Farewell, farewell! but this I tell
To thee, thou Wedding-Guest!
He prayeth well, who loveth well
Both man and bird and beast.

He prayeth best, who loveth best
All things both great and small;

For the dear God who loveth us,
He made and loveth all.

A simple Christian moral message is central here. You might, however, feel that these lines wrap everything up too neatly. This is because the poem as a whole has included disturbing details and disturbing features which work against the desire to find a consoling significance in the events narrated. The overall pattern is important, though, for again it enables the poet to maintain a wavering balance between our sense of the complexity of experience and our desire to find a meaning in experience. It is in the gap and tension between these that so much of the interest of poetry exists.

5   *Sum up your sense of the poem as a whole, and your sense of the writer so far*

Elsewhere in this book, I have looked at enough of a writer's poems to piece together some kind of overall picture of his work. At this point, however, with only a certain amount established, I want to call a halt to my discussion of Coleridge, because the note I want to end this chapter on is not a discussion of an individual writer but a summing-up of some points about difficult poetry. I have looked at very different writers here, but there are ways in which they have a great deal in common. In particular, there is a wavering tension in their work: they seem to acknowledge both the complexity of experience and the precarious quality of any order that is established. Different writers will achieve this in different ways, but essentially it is complications in imagery (or symbolism) and in structure that introduce a sense of diversity and complexity in a poem. Yet, at the same time, the poet is establishing a structure, and images do suggest that links can be established between different ideas of experience. At any particular point in a poem, therefore, we might simultaneously feel both the complexity of experience and the poet's compulsion towards understanding. What I have said in this chapter about difficult poetry must to a large extent apply to all poetry, but it is I think fair to say that it is only the most ambitious and gifted poets who make us feel that we are for ever simplifying their work if we try to pin it down.

# 5

# Narrative poetry

NARRATIVE poetry is poetry that tells a story. Poems can be divided into two main groups, lyric and narrative. Most of the poems we have looked at so far are lyrics. The exceptions are Pope's poems and Coleridge's 'The Ancient Mariner'. In the *Epistle to Dr Arbuthnot* Pope adapts the epistle, a form that is more commonly associated with prose-writing, and uses it as a verse form. *The Rape of the Lock*, *The Dunciad* and 'The Ancient Mariner' are narrative poems. The rest of the poems I have looked at are best described as lyrics: that is to say, as poems in which the poet offers his own direct response to some aspect of experience – for example, the death of a friend or falling in love. There are poems that are actually called lyrics, but the term 'lyric' is also the general term for most non-narrative poems, including such specific forms as the sonnet, the ode and the elegy.

The main forms of narrative poetry are the epic, the ballad and the romance. Poets do not always want to offer their immediate and self-revealing response to life, as is the case in lyric poetry, preferring to explore their ideas through the medium of a story. The reason for devoting a separate chapter to narrative poetry is that it can often prove harder to discuss than lyric poetry. Consider the example of Keats, who is best known for a handful of odes and a roughly equal number of narrative poems. When students first encounter his odes they might be unsure what to say, but they do usually realise that important themes are being explored. When you first read one of Keats's narrative poems, however, you might well enjoy the story, but be left with the feeling that it is just a story and does not therefore have the kind of larger significance that we look for in a lyric poem. This can lead to the idea that Keats's narrative poems are somehow less weighty or important than his odes, and it is all too easy to carry this assumption into essay-writing, where the temptation is simply to tell the poem's story, as if the line-by-line texture of a narrative poem is less complex than that of a lyric poem.

If you think about it, this kind of response must be wrong. Narrative poetry, far from being a less demanding mode, must be just as exciting as lyric, and all the usual poetic qualities of concentrated writing and complexity of meaning must be in evidence. But how do we find complex meanings when the natural response is just to summarise the story and imply that the significance of the poem can be seen in the summary? What we need is an approach to narrative poetry that gets us beyond merely retelling the story and allows us to do justice to its line-by-line texture. It is such an approach that I illustrate in the following pages; much of what I say will be a continuation of everything that I have said in previous chapters, but there are some ideas that help specifically with narrative verse. Rather than spell out these ideas here, I will introduce them in the following analysis of Keats's 'The Eve of St Agnes'. After I have established these ideas, and after a brief comment on Chaucer, I shall then, in the second half of this chapter, offer some suggestions about how to tackle the most ambitious of all English narrative poems, Milton's *Paradise Lost*.

## John Keats

The first thing you need to do with any narrative poem is read it through as a whole. It is always necessary to read and reread a poem, so on a first reading I would endeavour merely to discover what happens in the story. It is a good idea to write out a brief summary. In 'The Eve of St Agnes', for example, Keats tells the story of Madeline and her lover Porphyro. The poem takes place on St Agnes' Eve, when maidens have visions of their lovers or future husbands. Madeline is preparing to go to bed when Porphyro arrives at her house; his family and Madeline's are enemies and it is therefore dangerous for him to be there. However, an old nurse, Angela, is his friend, and she conceals him in Madeline's bedroom. In the middle of the night he joins Madeline, and early next morning they leave together. It is possible to finish the poem feeling that it is very prettily written but that it is just an exercise in story-telling. We cannot leave things there, however; we need to discover whether there is more substance to the poem, and the only way to discover this is to start looking at, and thinking about, the evidence.

1   *Look for a central opposition in the poem*

Just as with a lyric poem, we can start by searching for an opposition. We could concentrate on the opening lines, but it is also possible to search for an opposition in the story as a whole. This might sound difficult, but it becomes a lot easier if we have some idea about what we are looking for. To this end, it helps if we devote a few moments to thinking about the concept of a story. Think about some of the first stories we encounter in life, such as parables in the Bible and children's fables. These are stories that make a point; the fable of 'The Tortoise and the Hare', for example, uses a story to make the point that steady application will be rewarded. The story is constructed with this moral design in view. In a lot of stories, the good or deserving triumph in the end. What provides the tension and real interest in a story are all the problems along the way, but in the vast majority of stories things move steadily towards a happy conclusion. Stories, therefore, impose a consoling and positive pattern upon experience. The writer presents a dramatic situation built on conflict and tension, with threats and danger in evidence all along the way, but contrives things so that the eventual outcome is reassuring.

The concept of a story is, therefore, very much like the notion of poetic order that we have looked at in the earlier chapters of this book. The poet writing a narrative poem imposes the shape and order of a story upon experience. In more complex stories, however, there are a great many complications along the way, and even the eventual outcome might be unhappy. The reason is that the writer is allowing the disorder of life to undercut and disrupt a neat story. With such stories we again have a pattern, like that in poetry as a whole, of the complexity of experience challenging the poet's desire for order. This can be seen in 'The Ancient Mariner', which I discussed in the last chapter: when we summarise the story of 'The Ancient Mariner' it seems to be a simple moral fable about the need to respect all life, but the strangeness of the events and details along the way force us to consider a sense of experience that is so mysterious that it undercuts any neat moral pattern in the poem. All narrative poetry could be said to work in this kind of way: the poet tells a story, which can be seen to have a point and purpose, but the details of the poem force us to confront the complexity and disorder of experience. The two sides are held in tension: we are made to feel the complexity of the world, but we also share the artist's desire for a significant pattern in experience.

How does this relate to 'The Eve of St Agnes'? If we have managed to realise even as little as the fact that Keats is telling a love story, then we have already made substantial progress towards grasping its characteristics as a poem. A love story is one of the most popular kinds of story, for it offers a vision of a form of happiness that is not only glorious but also practical, in that it can actually be achieved in life. This, in its simplest form, is what Keats offer in 'The Eve of St Agnes': two lovers are brought together, and remain together at the end of the poem. For the poem to work, however, there has to be some kind of conflict in evidence; the most obvious thing that is set against love is Madeline's family's hostility towards Porphyro and his family. What this suggests is a tension in the poem between an ideal of love and the harsh realities of life; it is as if the untidiness and unpleasantness of the real world disrupt the neatness of a story. The effect, however, is not entirely disruptive: in good narrative poetry, as in good poetry generally, we are likely to be struck by a wavering tension between a sense of the complexity of experience and a desire for meaning and significance in experience; in 'The Eve of St Agnes', love represents the only sign of joy and hope in the atmosphere of aggression, waste and death that exists in Madeline's home.

It would be a naïve poem that let love triumph too easily, and by the same token a disappointingly pessimistic poem that painted a picture of a world where love was never allowed to blossom. There has to be a sense of love flourishing despite all the problems it has to face. What might disappoint us in 'The Eve of St Agnes', however, is the absence of clearly presented scenes of conflict. The story being told is very similar to that in Shakespeare's *Romeo and Juliet*, but in Shakespeare's play the hostility that exists between the two families is forcefully brought to life on the stage. In much the same way, Shakespeare also presents inspiring love scenes between Romeo and Juliet. In Keats's poem, however, we should search in vain for a real love scene between Madeline and Porphyro. Indeed, they are barely established as individual characters, and the poem seems lacking in action and character interest. It is therefore reasonable to feel that, although the poem is built on a tension, it lacks force in bringing that tension to life. I mentioned above the impression we might form that it is a prettily written poem, but not much more, and possibly this is true – that it is attractive but lacks tension. It might be the case, however, that I am approaching the poem in the wrong way, in expecting to find dramatic qualities of action and characterisation; a narrative poem might carry and express its concerns in a more subtle way in the texture of the verse. This is something we shall only discover, however, if we turn to the text.

2   *Begin to look at the details of the poem, trying to see how the poet brings his theme to life*

We can begin to see how a narrative poem carries and expresses its concerns if we look at the opening lines of the 'The Eve of St Agnes':

> St Agnes' Eve – ah, bitter chill it was!
> The owl, for all his feathers, was a-cold;
> The hare limped trembling through the frozen grass,
> And silent was the flock in woolly fold.
> Numb were the Beadsman's fingers, while he told
> His rosary, and while his frosted breath,
> Like pious incense from a censer old,
> Seemed taking flight for heaven, without a death,
> Past the sweet Virgin's picture, while his prayer he saith.

An opposition might not be immediately apparent here, but as I have said in earlier chapters, an opposition can sometimes be implicit rather than explicit, and yet it can still affect us. In these opening lines, what is likely to strike us is the chilling and hostile atmosphere created. What is lacking is any sense of warmth in life. And that really gives us a sense of the theme of the poem, the need for warmth, or love, in a cold world. This is never stated, of course, but the images convey this impression.

The images, therefore, announce the theme of the poem. And from the outset they are functioning in a complex way that adds to and constantly broadens the meaning of the poem. When, for example, Keats uses the images of cold animals and when he introduces religious imagery, he is establishing all kinds of complex ramifications of his theme. We begin to acquire a sense of a coldness that permeates all nature, and in addition form a view of a world where coldness is immediate while religious consolation seems remote. As it is images conveying these ideas, however, I must remind you of the fact that the images will convey different ideas to different readers, as meanings are being suggested rather than stated. It is obviously essential in discussing a poem that you try to describe as clearly as possible what the images convey to you, for it is only in that way that you can hope to establish your own individual reading of a poem. One thing that strikes me here, for example, is the image of the owl being cold despite his feathers and then the image of the 'flock in woolly fold'; it is a kind of inner coldness that is being described. I can see a link between this and Madeline, who is at home with her family but not experiencing the warmth of a family. She is alone, isolated and cold. And there does not seem to be any easy answer, for, when the Beadsman prays, religious comfort seems very far away.

Even within the space of the opening stanza, a great deal has been established. What is particularly important to note, however, is how the images function in a poem such as this. They are not there just to establish the setting in which the events of the poem will take place. On the contrary, they are making a far more active contribution to the poem by establishing the theme of the poem, and every additional image adds to the complexity and subtlety of the theme. So, when Keats refers to the limping hare, that prepares us for seeing Madeline as a vulnerable young woman in a harsh world, and also, in more general terms, touches on the frailty of any concept of happiness or love in such a world. Each stanza of the poem will add additional layers and implications of meaning, so that, as we go on, we are likely to feel that we are being offered a complex and convincing sense of the problems that beset not only the people in this poem but people in life generally.

As critics, however, we cannot hope to pick up and record every nuance of meaning suggested by every image. We can, though, concentrate on a few stanzas from the poem, and, in attempting to do justice to these stanzas, we shall find ourselves constructing a convincing and detailed impression of the poem as a whole. At this stage, therefore, it becomes necessary to pick another stanza for analysis. The verse I have selected deals with the arrival of Porphyro, but any stanza would prove just as rewarding to examine. What you would find in a stanza would be different from what I find in it, but that is how it should be; the analysis of poetry involves an individual reader putting together her or his own sense and analysis of the poem. And, just in case it is not apparent, what I am saying about a method for tackling 'The Eve of St Agnes' will work as a method for any narrative poem: search for the big theme in the poem, and then look at brief extracts, seeing how the poet brings his theme to life. As you do this, you will find yourself developing an acute awareness of the poem as a whole.

I hope this is apparent in the discussion of this stanza, which presents the arrival of Porphyro:

> He ventures in – let no buzzed whisper tell,
> All eyes be muffled, or a hundred swords
> Will storm his heart, love's feverous citadel.
> For him, those chambers held barbarian hordes,
> Hyena foemen, and hot-blooded lords,
> Whose very dogs would execrations howl
> Against his lineage; not one breast affords
> Him any mercy, in that mansion foul,
> Save one old beldame, weak in body and in soul.

What strikes me in this stanza is how aggressive images are set against soft images; this adds to the sense of the frailty of the innocent in a harsh world. In the previous stanza we looked at, Keats used images of meek and vulnerable animals, but on this occasion the animal imagery is unpleasant. There is the ugliness of the 'hyena', and the howling dogs. This sense of aggression in the world is also conveyed in the use of military imagery of swords and barbarian hordes. What is set against all this is a sense of delicacy, in the ideas of speaking in a whisper and eyes being muffled. This sustains, but also adds to, the idea of physical vulnerability in an aggressive world. It is not too fanciful to say that we are reading not just the story of Madeline and Porphyro but a broader consideration of the concept of love in a world where death and killing exist. None of this is stated of course, but the imagery is working to convey a larger implicit meaning in the poem. And what should be apparent by now is that a narrative poem does not necessarily need lots of action or complex characters, as the meanings of the poem are largely conveyed through the texture of the verse. That is why we always need to look closely at sections of the verse to acquire a full sense of what a poem is about.

3   *Look at another section of the poem, trying to see how the poem is
   progressing*

I have been pointing to the ways in which the poet can introduce
subtlety and complexity in his telling of a story. There is, to my
mind, this kind of complexity evident in the presentation of
Madeline and Porphyro. If we just summarise their story they are
the good lovers in an evil world, but when we look closely at the
verse we get, I think, a far more troubling and puzzling sense of the
two lovers. The first stanza in which this feeling struck me was the
one where Porphyro asked Angela to conceal him in Madeline's
chamber. Rather than talk in general terms about the significance
of this verse, it is obviously (as always) much more sensible to work
from the evidence of the stanza itself. Here, then, is Porphyro
putting his request to Angela:

> Which was to lead him, in close secrecy,
> Even to Madeline's chamber, and there hide
> Him in a closet, of such privacy
> That he might see her beauty unespied,
> And win perhaps that night a peerless bride,
> While legioned fairies paced her coverlet
> And pale enchantment held her sleepy-eyed.
> Never on such a night have lovers met
> Since Merlin paid his Demon all the monstrous debt.

The innocence and purity of Madeline is unmistakable here, but
there is something troubling in the idea of Porphyro spying on her
from a closet. I am also struck by the fact that the word 'win',
when Keats writes about Porphyro's winning a peerless bride,
seems to suggest a slight sense of military conquest. In addition,
the last few lines touch on magic and witchcraft, again seeming to
import a disturbing note into the stanza. Can you see how all these
details complicate the picture? The basic tension in the poem might
be love versus a cruel and nasty world, but complications are being
suggested within the very concept of love.

A look at another stanza might enable me to develop a clearer
sense of where all this is leading. This is the description of Porphyro
coming to Madeline's bed:

And still she slept an azure-lidded sleep,
In blanchèd linen, smooth and lavendered,
While he from forth the closet brought a heap
Of candied apple, quince, and plum, and gourd,
With jellies soother than the creamy curd,
And lucent syrops, tinct with cinnamon;
Manna and dates, in argosy transferred
From Fez; and spicèd dainties, every one,
From silken Samarcand to cedared Lebanon.

All the words describing Madeline, who is sleeping in 'smooth and lavendered' linen, are clean and pure. This, I think, makes it clear how all the images associated with Porphyro here are too rich and lush. It is apparent in the long list of exotic, sticky sweets; all of them seem to involve taking the natural item, such as an apple, and transforming it with a syrup or spice. All of this might seem hard to understand at first, but what we have to remember is that the significance of such lines must be consistent with what we have already discovered about the theme of the poem, and what we have discovered is that Keats faces up to the complex nature of existence. Here, I feel, Keats is hinting at the complexity of love, that Porphyro might be motivated by love but his feelings incorporate entrapment, seduction, passion and lust; the stanza offers a troubling sense of sexual passion which might be a part of, but which is not quite the same thing as, love. The purity of Madeline is evident, but she in a sense is caught between two extremes: the harsh coldness of her family and the excessive warmth of Porphyro.

The effect I have spotted here, although developed by Keats in a particular direction, is an effect that can be found in a lot of narrative poems. The basic tension is simple, but, as the poem develops, the writer incorporates more and more details, giving an ever-growing sense of the complexity of experience. At the heart of a narrative poem might be a simple sense of how things should be in an ideal world, but the poem manages to acknowledge the variety and complexity of the real world. Yet a concept such as love is still important, for, even though it may be presented as frail, precarious and under threat, it stands for something positive in a chilling or disturbing world.

Much of what I am saying is economically illustrated in the following stanza, which starts with a description of Porphyro:

Beyond a mortal man impassioned far
At these voluptuous accents, he arose,
Ethereal, flushed, and like a throbbing star
Seen mid the sapphire heaven's deep repose;
Into her dream he melted, as the rose
Blendeth its odour with the violet,
Solution sweet – meantime the frost-wind blows
Like Love's alarum pattering the sharp sleet
Against the window-panes; St Agnes' moon hath set.

At the heart of the stanza is a simple, pure notion of love, conveyed in the simple nature imagery of the rose blending with the violet. But this is surrounded by complications. At the end of the stanza it is the sharp coldness of the world at large, conveyed in the images of frost and sleet, that challenges the simple notion of love. At the beginning of the stanza, however, the troubling note is much more complicated: Keats presents a flushed, throbbing sense of Porphyro.

### 4    *Look at how the poem concludes*

The two lovers flee together; in summary, this is an uncomplicated, positive ending, but I do not think that such a straightforward impression comes across from the poem. You would need to look at the closing stanzas, particularly at lines such as those which describe them gliding 'like phantoms' as they leave, to decide quite what effect is created. To my mind, however, there is, through to the end of the poem, a sense of something unsettling that disrupts the neat fiction of two people in love.

### 5    *Sum up your sense of the poem as a whole, and your sense of the writer so far*

I think I have established that 'The Eve of St Agnes' is a complex and complicated poem, far more complex than might initially appear to be the case. There is, however, something very straightforward about the way in which it becomes complex, for what Keats does is disrupt the neat, consoling pattern of a story. The poem makes us confront the complexity of experience, but what makes it so special is the particular images Keats chooses which convey his own unique sense of the nature of experience. In particular, Keats's use of imagery in this poem conveys a disturbing sense of Porphyro's sexual feelings, and, more generally, a sense of a chilling and rather frightening world. Love might strike us as a frail concept in such a world, but we end the poem torn between a sense of the complexity of experience and a desire for a simple order in experience. We can expect to find much the same pattern in most narrative poems: an unresolved tension between the neatness of the story and the complexity of experience. As the next section of this chapter tries to show, this tension is in evidence in even the longest and most ambitious narrative poems.

## Geoffrey Chaucer

The two greatest English narrative poems are Chaucer's *Canterbury Tales* and Milton's *Paradise Lost*. Poems as long as these are daunting, but length is not the greatest problem we face when we study either of them for the first time. The overwhelming difficulty is that both poems are difficult to read. With Chaucer, there is the obvious problem that he is a medieval poet, which means that his language, although having quite a lot in common with modern English, can prove a barrier. We do not need to translate Milton's *Paradise Lost* in the same way as we have to translate Chaucer, but Milton's style is so inflated and his sentence structure so complicated that he can prove almost as difficult to read as Chaucer. With either writer you could well feel that you are floundering. This is unfortunate, as many students thus come to regard Milton and Chaucer as authors they are obliged to study rather than as writers they actually enjoy reading. Something has clearly gone wrong when studying two of the best English poets seems more of a chore than a pleasure.

If, however, we could arrive fairly quickly at a broad understanding of what Chaucer and Milton are doing in, respectively, *The Canterbury Tales* and *Paradise Lost*, some of the problems of understanding the line-by-line progress of their works might disappear, for understanding of the works as a whole is bound to make it easier to come to terms with the details of the works. Fortunately, the method I have described for tackling a fairly short narrative poem such as 'The Eve of St Agnes' will work just as well with Chaucer and Milton. It will not tell us everything we need to know, but it will allow us to get a confident grasp on either writer. I have not got enough space to deal in detail with

both Chaucer and Milton, but shall try to provide a few pointers
for *The Canterbury Tales* here.

What happens in the poem is that a group of pilgrims on their
way to Canterbury tell tales to divert and entertain their fellow
travellers. If you have to study one or more of these tales, you
might well discover that, once you have found out what happens,
you are at a loss as to what to say about it. At this point, it can
help if you start making use of the ideas I have presented in this
chapter. Start by summarising the story; you should find that it is a
simple story with a fairly obvious moral point. There must,
however, be more to Chaucer's purpose than just providing a
sequence of straightforward moral tales. Ask yourself, therefore,
whether the story you have just read is as neat and simple as it
seems in your summary. One possible complication is that the
teller of the story might be telling a moral tale which is at odds
with his or her character; a lustful character, for example, the Wife
of Bath, might tell a story about the wickedness of lust. Such a
discrepancy is interesting because it points to that gap between
how things should be in an ideal world and how they really are; the
disorder of experience undercuts the moral pattern of the story. It
is, however, not just the teller of the tale who complicates the
pattern. The details of the story, the evidence it provides about the
complexity of life and human nature, will also suggest that life is
more complex than neat fiction.

This is crystallised in a concept Chaucer made frequent use of,
the concept of courtly love, the man worships the woman from a
distance. It is an ideal passion, never tainted by self-interest or
corrupted desire. In those stories, such as 'The Franklin's Tale',
that make use of the notion of courtly love, however, human
failings, in particular the sexual needs of the individual involved,
undermine the ideal standard. As in other good poems, therefore,
we are thrown back onto the complexity of experience. But a poem
does not just throw us back onto the muddle of life. We can
appreciate this if we think about the group of pilgrims on their way
to Canterbury; here is a diverse group of people, many of whom
have numerous failings, but the idea of the pilgrimage does suggest
a larger purpose and design in experience. This provides us with a
way of talking about the Prologue to *The Canterbury Tales*: the
Prologue is built on the tension between the idea of a significant
religious journey and a group of fallible individuals, many of whom
have, in their moral standards, fallen by the wayside. There is

again, as in so much poetry, a wavering tension between the diffuse complexity of experience and a sense of a larger order that the poet seeks, or perceives, in experience. There is, in fact, a very simple way of describing this kind of tension as it appears in narrative poetry: this is to talk about the difference between the story and the discourse – that is, the actual language of the poem. The story is neat and purposeful; it seems to reflect the notion of a significant order in experience. The discourse, however, endlessly complicates and undermines such a neat structure. In Chaucer, the tension is often as simple as the gap between the complex varieties of human weakness and a simple religious, moral ideal.

We can see this if we take just one example from the Prologue, Chaucer's description of the prioress. This covers some thirty lines and is too long for me to discuss in full here, but let me give you a brief summary. Chaucer describes the Prioress, Madame Eglentyne, as a fine singer; she has nice manners, is pleasant company, shows tender feelings towards animals and is attractively dressed. Can you see how there is, even in this summary, a gap between the idea of the Prioress as a figure from a religious order and the human reality of her secular attributes? And yet Chaucer does not crudely condemn the Prioress, but leaves us our judgements. He does this largely through the details of the portrait he includes. For example, he ends his description of the Prioress by noting that she wears a gold brooch, and that on it is engraved the Latin motto '*Amor vincit omnia*'. Don't be put off by the Latin here: it simply means 'Love conquers all'. What sort of love, heavenly or earthly, Chaucer does not say; he leaves us instead with that sort of ambivalent uncertainty that I have described as characterising all great poetry, an uncertainty which reflects the richness of great poetry.

## John Milton

An approach to *Paradise Lost* can be built upon the principles I have described so far. *Paradise Lost* tells the story of Satan being thrown out of heaven, his descent into hell, his tempting of Eve, and the expulsion of Adam and Eve from the Garden of Eden. All is not lost, however, for Christ can deliver people from their fallen state. What is the purpose and point of such a story? The purpose is simple: we live in a fallen world where sin and death exist. The poem sets out to illustrate how there is a divine order in life. To express this in even briefer terms: *Paradise Lost* is a poem about God's love in a world where sin and death exist. If the intention of the poem is as clear as this, however, you might wonder why Milton has written such an immensely long poem. The answer is that the poem has a clear-cut purpose, but it is also a complex purpose, for Milton desires to do justice to the immense complexity of experience. The poem is an epic, which is a poem that sets out to confront and make sense of the whole of experience. It therefore has to be immense because of the range of its picture of life; and, just as it is immense in its range, so the poet's ambition is huge, for he attempts to present a coherent view of life in which he seeks to explain an order, in this case a divine order, in the whole of experience. The manner in which Milton fulfils these ambitious goals, if he does indeed fulfil them, should start to become clear as we look at the opening of the poem.

1   *Look for a central opposition in the poem*

*Paradise Lost* is such an immense poem that I can obviously only hope to provide a few pointers about how to proceed. As always, however, the method I describe should get you quite a long way with the poem; it should help you with whatever passages or whatever books of the poem you choose to or are required to study. What I am going to do here is look at a few brief sections of Book I, and then take a very quick look at a passage from Book IX. The poem opens as follows:

> Of man's first disobedience, and the fruit
> Of that forbidden tree, whose mortal taste
> Brought death into the world, and all our woe,
> With loss of Eden, till one greater Man
> Restore us, and regain the blissful seat,
> Sing, heavenly Muse, that on the secret top
> Of Oreb, or of Sinai, didst inspire
> That shepherd who first taught the chosen seed
> In the beginning how the heavens and earth
> Rose out of Chaos; or if Sion hill
> Delight thee more, and Siloa's brook that flowed
> Fast by the oracle of God, I thence
> Invoke thy aid to my adventurous song,
> That with no middle flight intends to soar

Above the Aonian mount, while it pursues
Things unattempted yet in prose or rhyme.

This opening sentence of the poem is sixteen lines long, and it is obviously an immensely complicated sentence. It is just this kind of complication of structure, and the difficulty of grasping all that is being said, that can confuse or alienate the reader encountering *Paradise Lost* for the first time. In a moment, however, we shall try to find a reason why Milton writes such a long opening sentence; if we can come to terms with this it should make it much easier to cope with a whole variety of aspects of the poem.

First, though, we need to look for an opposition in the hope that this will enable us to identify the central theme in the poem. It is, in fact, not all that difficult, as Milton does state his theme fairly directly here. Milton is going to look at the problems of disobedience, sin and death. And he immediately provides us with the solution: the 'greater Man' he refers to is Christ, and it is Christ who will restore us to the kingdom of heaven. We might worry about death but we can feel secure in the knowledge of God's love. A few lines later Milton tells us that he hopes to justify the ways of God to man: the same note is struck again, therefore, that he will examine and explain God's divine plan for the world.

I think it is fair to say that when we look at that opening declaration of a purpose we might wonder whether *Paradise Lost* will really prove to be a complex poem, for everything does seem settled and resolved even before the poem starts. I have talked throughout this book about tension between a complex sense of experience and poetry's desire to find an order in experience; the reservation we might have here is that, according to this opening sentence, Milton seems only concerned to illustrate and explain the concept of God's order. To get beyond that feeling, however, it is necessary to return to our initial response to this opening sentence; as I have already said, the sentence goes on for so long and becomes so convoluted that we are likely to feel lost within seconds of starting the poem. In some ways, therefore, it is a reassuring sentence, but only when we have worked out what Milton is saying. Initially it appears to be a baffling and taxing sentence. The point to grasp is that the complication of structure is part of the meaning of the poem: the sentence goes on and on, bewildering us with a sense of the complexity of the world. It is only by the most astonishing effort that Milton manages to impose overall control on the diverse materials of this sentence. And in that we have, in miniature, a sense of what the poem as a whole is going to be like and what it is going to be about. On the one hand, the poem will consistently expand and become more complicated, giving an immense vision of the complex nature of experience. Yet we shall always be conscious of the poet managing to exert his authority and control. Milton does not give himself an easy ride, however: the poem maintains a sense of the world's disorder, which is complex and confusing enough to challenge Milton's desire to find and impose coherence. The poem might set out to justify the ways of God to men, but the approach Milton adopts involves presenting such a complex sense of experience that any greater truth he reveals will have to encompass and contain all those complex facts about life and the history of mankind.

When you study the poem, whatever book or books you focus on, one of the main things to concentrate on is how Milton creates an impression of a disorder that challenges his impulse towards creating an order. That immediately makes it a lot easier to talk about any individual extract, it gives you something to look for. It also gives you a way of explaining many of the details that you will encounter, for you can always argue that the diffuse and varied details create an impression of a complex and disordered universe. All of this should become apparent as we take a closer look at another extract from the poem.

2 *Begin to look at the details of the poem, trying to see how the poet brings his theme to life*

The principal events in Book I of *Paradise Lost* are Satan's rallying of the fallen angels after their defeat by God and his declaration that he will fight against God in every possible way. As Satan is so central in Book I, it obviously makes sense to look at him here. I shall start with the first reference to him in the poem:

> The infernal serpent; he it was whose guile,
> Stirred up with envy and revenge, deceived
> The mother of mankind, what time his pride
> Had cast him out from heaven, with all his host
> Of rebel angels, by whose aid aspiring
> To set himself in glory above his peers,
> He trusted to have equalled the Most High,

If he opposed; and with ambitious aim
Against the throne and monarchy of God
Raised impious war in heaven and battle proud
With vain attempt. Him the Almighty Power
Hurled headlong flaming from the ethereal sky
With hideous ruin and combustion down
To bottomless perdition, there to dwell
In adamantine chains and penal fire . . . .

The first thing that struck me in reading this passage is the way in which so many nouns seem to be coupled with an appropriate adjective, as in 'infernal serpent', 'impious war', 'hideous ruin' and 'bottomless perdition'. This is the kind of thing I might well have noticed when I was studying *Paradise Lost* at school, but then not known what to say about the feature I had spotted. It is a familiar feeling in criticism, not knowing how to transform an observation about the text into a worthwhile point about the text. The answer, however, is simple. Every detail will either be contributing to a sense of disorder in experience or will reflect order in some way. Let us look, then, at these adjective-and-noun phrases. On one level they clearly reflect disorder: they refer to the serpent, war, ruin and perdition. It would be hard to envisage a more extreme list of problems and woes. There is, however, a force pulling in the opposite direction: the regularity with which Milton supplies an appropriate descriptive adjective for the noun suggests a writer who is imposing some kind of regularity and control upon his materials. This becomes even more obvious if we think about the predictability of the adjectives; it is the most obvious thing in the world to refer to the serpent as the 'infernal serpent'. The effect of such predictable adjective–noun combinations every couple of lines is to suggest an author who has got the measure of even the most extreme problems. It is as if the truth is encapsulated in received phrases and that Milton can exert order and control over even the most extreme concepts.

In essence, then, we have a picture of Satan who is the embodiment of evil and disorder, but also a sense of a writer who has got the measure of this evil force. And there are other ways in which Milton reveals his control. There is, for example, a confident and comprehensive listing of Satan's faults, all of which centre in the one area of sins of immoderation and lack of discipline: we are told that he is guilty of guile, envy, revenge, pride and ambition.

Can you see how all these are faults of wanting to disrupt an inherited order, of not accepting his place in the scheme of things? Indeed, because the problem is this rebelliousness and disobedience, it becomes essential that Milton appears firmly in charge. Through his own verse he must announce a sense of discipline, order and control. Milton must make it plain that he has a sense of order in experience which is large enough to contain and neutralise the disorderly impulse in existence.

It is, however, a fairly precarious control, for the disorderly forces are so strong. In addition, there is also a sense of a very large universe that Milton is attempting to make sense of and explain. This is apparent in the way that Satan is flung out of heaven and descends from the greatest height to the lowest depths. Just as the issues are enormous, so too the sense of space is enormous, yet what also comes across in the poem is a sense of a writer who can conceive of and control action on a massive scale. There is an almost arrogant confidence in the way that he presents this picture of war in the heavens. It is as if he understands and has got the measure of the most extraordinary events. The control is exercised through his control of the sentences; the lines beginning 'Him the almighty power . . . ' push 'Him', referring to Satan, into a commanding position at the start of the sentence, but as the sentence continues we can see that he has been defeated and expelled from heaven. It is as if a massive force of evil is being confronted and dominated.

Again, however, we might return to the question of whether there is a real tension in the poem, for God and Milton seem so firmly in control. Yet there is always, I feel, a sense of Satan as so powerful that he seems almost too big and powerful to control. We might be aware of Milton's control, but we are also aware of Satan's force. This sense of his force and indeed of other aspects of his personality become more apparent as we look at a passage, such as the following from later in Book I, where we see him speaking and rallying his fellow rebels:

Seest thou yon dreary plain, forlorn and wild,
The seat of desolation, void of light,
Save what the glimmering of these livid flames
Casts pale and dreadful? Thither let us tend
From off the tossing of these fiery waves,
There rest, if any rest can harbour there,

And reassembling our afflicted powers,
Consult how we may henceforth most offend
Our enemy, our own loss how repair,
How overcome this dire calamity,
What reinforcement we may gain from hope,
If not what resolution from despair.

My impression is that a fairly favourable image of Satan comes across from these lines. We can almost sympathise with rebels who have been flung into a 'dreary plain, forlorn and wild', and there is not only energy but also a kind of bravery in Satan's words as he refuses to accept defeat. He is, of course, the incarnation of evil and entirely motivated by hate, and in a way his words graphically reveal such shortcomings, but none the less this is someone who leads, speaks to and inspires his forces in terms we can understand.

Can this, however, be a correct view of the poem? Are we really meant to sympathise with Satan? I think we are meant to see some admirable qualities in him, for if the poem is going to work we must be allowed to feel the strength of the force that works against God's order. The poem comes to life because we feel that there is a real tension. The presentation of Satan makes us feel that the force of Satan, including the tempting power of his speech, can barely be contained. A question that sometimes comes up in relation to *Paradise Lost* is whether Satan is the real hero of the poem. What underlies this suggestion is the sense that his refusal to submit to God's authority is courageous, even heroic, and that he is therefore a comprehensible character – unlike God, who must appear as an abstract and inhuman force. To suggest that Satan is the hero, however, is to impose too neat and reductive a reading on the poem. Rather than pursue the point at this stage, though, it should prove more productive if we discuss it in the light of a further extract.

3   *Look at another section of the poem, trying to see how the poem is
    progressing*

It is quite possible that a question about Satan's heroic qualities might be set in an exam. You could agree, and argue that he is courageous, or you could condemn him as utterly evil. Or, and this is the approach that I am taking, you could argue that the poem makes him attractive while at the same time condemning him. The great danger in answering such a question, however, is trying to prove your case merely from an account of the events and actions in the story. For an answer really to work – and this would apply to any question about *Paradise Lost* – you must prove your case from the actual evidence of the words of the poem. This is not too difficult, as all you need to do is select a short extract for close attention. Any passage in which Satan appears or speaks should provide you with plenty to say. For example, here are some more lines where he addresses his troops:

> Here at least
> We shall be free; the Almighty hath not built
> Here for his envy, will not drive us hence:
> Here we may reign secure, and in my choice
> To reign is worth ambition though in hell:
> Better to reign in hell, than serve in heaven.

This is another inspiring speech from Satan. He talks of freedom, and obviously prefers freedom in hell to servitude in heaven. Yet his words can also be viewed from another perspective: he begins by talking about how 'We shall be free', but within these few lines has shifted from this general concern for all his followers and is merely concerned with his own position as the leader who will 'reign in hell'. The same double-sided quality is also apparent in the very sound and texture of his words: his words can appear elevated, dignified and heroic, but they can also be judged as empty bombast. At times the manner of his speech almost resembles a salesman's clever play with words.

You might, by this stage, be confused about where all this is leading us, but the point I am making is one that I have made repeatedly in this book: that there is, in the greatest poetry, an unstable tension between a sense of order and a sense of disorder. *Paradise Lost* as a whole might be examining and explaining the concept of a divine order that operates in and shapes all experience, but it would be a very simple poem if it simply condemned out of hand anything and everything that challenges God's order. It therefore presents us with a vivid and even sympathetic sense of how and why people, and even fallen angels, are unruly, and must show us the attractions and temptations of rebellion and sin. There will, therefore, be a light in which Satan can appear as heroic, but by making his words specious Milton can simultaneously show the hollowness of everything Satan represents.

I have concentrated on the presentation of Satan in this book because this provides one of the easiest paths into the poem, but what I have said has a more general application and should help you in coming to terms with various qualities of the poem. There is always a sense of a real problem and a real tension in the poem. Milton cannot present a story in which he just provides a simple sense of God's providential order at work in existence. We have to be allowed to feel all the snarled complexity of life. And this should help us in understanding the tremendous complexity of the poem, such things as the range of reference and the complex structure of sentences. All these features help enact a sense of a diverse and complex world that is difficult to comprehend, let alone control. Yet we should also always be able to feel a precarious, elaborate control in the sentences and verse paragraphs of the poem as Milton, by a kind of superhuman effort, just manages to impose control. In reading the poem, you will not be going wrong if you feel that everything is so big that it is just about running out of control, but do also try to see how Milton does manage to hold everything together. Potentially everything is chaotic, yet there is simultaneously a strong sense of order always in evidence.

4    *Look at how the poem concludes*

Book I ends with the followers of Satan congregating:

> So thick the airy crowd
> Swarmed and were straitened; till the signal given,
> Behold a wonder! they but now who seemed
> In bigness to surpass Earth's giant sons
> Now less than smallest dwarfs, in narrow room
> Throng numberless, like that Pygmean race
> Beyond the Indian mount . . . .

I think the dual effect I have been describing, of Satan being both impressive yet hollow, is, in a slightly different way, again in evidence here. If we read these lines, paying attention perhaps primarily to their sound and just forming a casual impression of what is being said, then we are likely to feel that there is something awe-inspiring about this grand gathering of rebels. Here is a numberless throng gathering together to challenge God; in fact, Milton inverts the phrase, as he does so often in the poem, calling them a 'Throng numberless' and the effect of this inversion, as is the case everywhere in the poem, is that it makes everything seem elevated. Milton departs from the everyday construction, and by doing so conveys a sense of something special that surpasses everyday concerns. The lines convey to us an impression of throbbing, restless energy, of a great force that is going to rise up against God and provoke tremendous unrest.

Yet look at the same time at all the rather sly ways in which Milton makes these rebels seem petty and insignificant. He compares them to bees swarming, and as they make themselves small so that they can all be contained in one place Milton seizes the opportunity to refer to them as dwarfs and pygmies. The effect, as always, is that we feel the scale of the problem that is being confronted in the poem yet also feel that Milton has a larger sense of a divine order in which all challenges to God's authority just become a part of God's larger plan for the world.

5   *Sum up your sense of the poem as a whole, and your sense of the writer so far*

What we have seen in Book I of *Paradise Lost* is how, as in all the greatest poetry, there is a wavering tension between a sense of the complexity and disorder of the world and a sense of order that the poet explores, seeks or perceives in experience. The disorderly fact is that we live in a fallen world; the answer, the source of order, is God.

Yet the mention of God, and the ease with which, in that last extract we considered, the rebels are scorned, might well make us wonder again whether there is really an uneasy tension in the poem. It could be argued that Milton makes Satan just appealing enough to make the poem interesting, but that he is very firmly in control all the time, confidently and consistently justifying the ways of God to men. The thing is, however, that when we read the poem I think we do feel the strength of the forces that are pulling in the opposite direction, and do feel that Milton is having to go to extreme lengths, just as his sentences often became extremely long, to hold everything together.

In addition, at perhaps the most crucial point in the whole

poem, it could be argued that God's order is questioned and possibly rejected. In Book IX, Eve is tempted by the serpent and tastes the forbidden fruit. She then tells Adam. In this following extract, we see him deciding what to do, whether to be loyal to God or whether to stay with and support Eve:

> Speechless he stood and pale, till thus at length
> First to himself he inward silence broke:
>     'O fairest of creation, last and best
> Of all God's works, creature in whom excelled
> Whatever can to sight or thought be formed,
> Holy, divine, good, amiable, or sweet!
> How art thou lost, how on a sudden lost,
> Defaced, deflowered, and now to death devote!
> Rather how hast thou yielded to transgress
> The strict forbiddance, how to violate
> The sacred fruit forbidden! Some cursèd fraud
> Of enemy hath beguiled thee, yet unknown,
> And me with thee hath ruined, for with thee
> Certain my resolution is to die;
> How can I live without thee, how forgo
> Thy sweet converse and love so dearly joined,
> To live again in these wild woods forlorn?
> Should God create another Eve, and I
> Another rib afford, yet loss of thee
> Would never from my heart; no, no! I feel
> The link of nature draw me: flesh of flesh,
> Bone of my bone thou art, and from thy state
> Mine never shall be parted, bliss or woe.'

I think this is a wonderful passage, as we see Adam's consternation, his turning in on himself and examination of his feelings, and his decision that his commitment to Eve must stand before even his commitment to God. In a poem that is so often cosmic in its range of reference and so often convoluted in its sentences, there is something strikingly beautiful in the plain simplicity of a line such as 'How can I live without thee . . . '. It is, then, an appealing passage, but I think also a very important one, for it does seem that personal commitment here surpasses even religious commitment. It could even be argued that, in a poem that sets out to justify the ways of God to men, this particular moment in the poem justifies the ways of men to God as it shows that, for Adam, human love is more important than divine love. That is not the last word that could be offered on this extract; it could be argued, for example, that this is again all part of a larger order in the poem. But the point I am concerned to make here is the point I have been making all along, that there is a tension at the heart of poetry and very often it is the case that this tension will not be resolved, that we shall come away from a poem with a sense of the complexity of experience set against the poet's desire to establish a sense of order in experience.

There is much more that could be said about *Paradise Lost*, as, of course, there is much more that could be said about all the poets that I have discussed in this book. In particular, when you study a poet in detail you will want to consider his or her works in context, you will want to see how they relate to and reflect the period in which they were written. And you will need to go into a poet's works in far greater detail than I have managed to do in this book. None the less, you should find that the kind of approach I have illustrated should enable you to make a solid start on the work of any writer. There is, however, one further issue that I still need to consider. English is a subject where you have to write essays. Your understanding of a writer will always be wasted if you are incapable of writing a good essay, and it is therefore to the topic of essay-writing that I turn in the final chapter.

# 6

## Essay-writing

IF you have studied a poet and enjoyed his or her work, then writing an essay about the author should be enjoyable. It is, after all, a chance for you to convey in your own words what you have found interesting and attractive in the poetry. The fact is, however, that most people find essay-writing extremely hard work, and most people are disappointed with their essays, often feeling that they have not quite managed to say what they wanted to say. Obviously I cannot hope to solve in this one chapter all the problems associated with writing essays. Writing is taxing, and time and time again the words just will not do what you want them to do. What I can offer, however, are some ideas that can help you get started, some guidance about what you are trying to do in an essay, and some tips about how to organise and structure your essays.

I have tried to make this chapter simple and straightforward, because the basic format of an essay should be simple and straightforward. Indeed, where most people go wrong is that they tie themselves up in knots, saying too many things at once, so that by the end of the essay they do not know what they are saying at all. It is a problem we have all experienced, and it is a problem that is bound to occur unless you develop a method for approaching and handling an essay. Our first rule of essay-writing, therefore, can be **rely on a method rather than trusting to inspiration**. I ought to expand on this just because the myth of 'inspiration' is such a problem. When you study a science subject you know that there are recognised formats for writing down and presenting your results. Some people would argue that English cannot be organised in this way, that, because a personal response is involved, no rules can be established about how that response should be controlled. And all of us are aware that there are times when the words flow more easily, times when we feel inspired. It is, however, no good waiting for inspiration to strike or you could find yourself waiting for ever. My favourite comment on this is by an author who says that he only writes when inspiration strikes, and he makes sure that it strikes at nine o'clock every morning. There is a lot of truth in this remark: you do not need to be in the right mood to write, nor do you need to wait while the thoughts sort themselves out in your mind before putting pen to paper. You can sit down at a desk at any time and start writing. But it will help if you know what you are trying to do in an essay and if you know how to construct an essay. It is this whole subject of how to build an essay that I turn to now.

The object of an essay can be summed up in the following formula: **in a critical essay you are trying to build a clear argument from the evidence of the text.** There are two points involved here that must remain at the front of your mind the whole time you are writing. One is that it is essential to keep on referring to the text or texts. Unsubstantiated assertions are of no value: you must keep pointing to the specific sections or lines in a poem that support what you are saying. The other point is the need to build an argument: this is something that many students find difficult, but it is very easy if you make use of paragraphing in your essay in an efficient way. The thing to tell yourself is that **each paragraph must advance the argument in an essay by a substantial step**. It helps if you start with a paragraph plan. By this I do not mean a detailed account of the material each paragraph will cover, merely a sense of the kind of overall format that might help produce a good essay. What I always do is think in terms of approximately eight paragraphs: one paragraph of introduction which sets the essay up, then six paragraphs which develop the argument, each paragraph advancing the case being made, and finally a short concluding paragraph which pulls together all the threads of the essay. It might help if I suggest approximate lengths for these paragraphs: a paragraph of about ten to twelve lines should be quite long enough to introduce the issue in an essay, and the paragraph of conclusion can be about the same length. The six paragraphs at the heart of the essay (it can be more or less than six) are likely to work best if they are about half to two-thirds of a side in length. Can you see how I am not only establishing a shape for an essay but also taking steps to guarantee that I write an essay that develops an argument? I am thinking very clearly in terms of paragraphs that advance an argument, and, if each paragraph at the heart of the essay is more or less the same length, then the argument is likely to advance in regular steps.

Look out for danger signs when you are writing an essay: if a paragraph goes on for too long it means that you are rambling. If you write in very short paragraphs what you have to say will not only *appear* bitty but also *be* bitty. Think of each paragraph as a natural, logical step in your thinking. I might seem to be spending a long time going on about something that is obvious, but the conventions about writing in structured paragraphs are all too often ignored by examination candidates. It is vital to appreciate that slackness in writing an essay in paragraphs can easily lead to failure, while just a touch of common sense about writing in paragraphs of fairly consistent length can transform what might have been an average essay into a very good essay. When an examiner picks up an examination paper, he or she can tell a lot just by looking at how the answers are presented. An essay that looks shapeless, or has no clear paragraph breaks, or too many short paragraphs, will usually turn out to be a weak essay. By contrast, an essay with substantial, clearly defined paragraphs gives an impression of a student who has organised and structured his or her work, and these disciplined qualities will almost invariably result in a good answer.

The whole notion of working in solid paragraphs is not, however, going to prove much use unless you have some idea about how to fill out each paragraph. It helps here if you think about **the kind of questions that are set about poetry**. Examination questions on poetry are often rather vague, particularly when compared to the questions that are set on novels and plays. The reason for this is that in novels and plays there are so many elements, such as character, plot, themes and language, that can be discussed that questions can be precisely focused. Questions on poetry are generally far less specific. From the point of view of the examination candidate, this is both a good thing and a bad thing. A fairly broad question gives you a great deal of freedom to write the answer you want to write (although you must make sure you are answering the question set), but the problem is that a rather unfocused question can lead to an unfocused answer where there is a temptation merely to describe rather than to argue a case. Tell yourself, therefore, that the question, however it is phrased, is confronting you with a problem about the writer, and in order to present your view you will have to argue a case about the writer. What, in fact, most questions about a poet ask for is for you to present your assessment of that writer. You are being asked to write an essay in which, by the final paragraph, you will have presented your sense of what the poet writes about and how he or she writes about it. To put it as concisely as possible, you are being asked to produce **your coherent and well-argued view of the poet**. The only qualification I would add here is that, although it is always essentially the same question that is being asked about poets, you must take care to answer the specific question set. You cannot go into an examination with a prepared answer which you simply pour out onto the page. If the question asks you to consider specific poems, then you must consider those poems, and, if the question asks you to look at particular aspects of an author's work, then you must look at those aspects. But do try to see how the concentration on specific poems or a particular topic is merely a way of focusing your overall impression of the writer, which should emerge in the course of your answer.

So in an essay or an exam you are answering a specific question but at the same time, in your answer, you are also building a view of the writer. A good essay format should help you handle all this in a confident way. An essay can start in a very simple manner, just defining the issue to be explored, but then each paragraph along the way should add something to the answer so that by the end a full sense of the author, of what he writes about and how he writes about it, is established. It is, however, only at the end of an essay that the full picture will have emerged. Do not therefore burden yourself with difficulties at the outset. In particular, take great pains to get your **first paragraph** right. The best thing to do in a first paragraph is to simply **introduce the problem or issue that is going to be examined**. You don't need to provide an answer yet. Merely introduce the problem in a straightforward manner: one way is to start with a superficial impression of the poet's work but then state that the rest of your essay will look more closely at the true nature of his work. If you were writing on Keats, for example, you might start by saying that his work is attractive and enjoyable to read, and that poems such as 'Ode to a Nightingale' and 'To Autumn' are very beautiful, but that there is obviously more to his work than just these surface qualities. You can then say that the rest of your essay will go on to explore and establish a fuller sense of his achievement. Can you see how this approach introduces the issue in a gentle but helpful way? You haven't confused yourself or your reader, and you have held out the considerable promise that by the end of the essay you will have established a full picture of the writer. It always helps in essay-writing if you remind yourself that you are writing for two people: you are writing for yourself, in order to sort out what you feel about a poet, but you are also writing for your reader. The reader of your essay is someone who must be treated with care: think of him or her as an elderly relative who has to be steered carefully along with everything along the way being explained in a clear voice.

A modest opening paragraph, such as I have described, will get your essay off to a clear and confident start. It also avoids the two problems that often occur at the start of an essay. One of those problems is that essays often start with two opening paragraphs: the candidate introduces the subject and then, not quite happy with what she or he has said, introduces it again in a second paragraph. It is almost invariably the case that an essay that rambles at the start in this kind of way will continue to ramble, whereas a controlled and disciplined opening paragraph will help you produce a controlled essay. The other danger at the beginning of an essay is writing a paragraph that contains too much information: you can't say all there is to say about a writer in your opening paragraph because there is a limit to how much information the reader of your essay can absorb at one go. If your first paragraph contains too many facts, too many ideas, and too many large statements about the author, then it will alienate your reader. He or she would much rather be steered into the subject in a gentle way; all the complications can be introduced as your essay develops.

Let us assume that you now have a brief opening paragraph that sets up the issue. You have defined your task: taking account of the question, you are going to start building a picture of the writer. What you need to establish in your **second paragraph** are your first ideas about the concerns at the heart of the poet's work. There are two ways of structuring this paragraph. You can either make a statement about the writer and then introduce examples to back up what you have said, or, and this is a far more fruitful approach, you can turn to a passage from a poem and **begin to build your view from the evidence of the text**. This is a sensible approach because it guarantees that you work from the author's actual words, and also helps you build your argument. The opening sentence of this paragraph can be very simple: for example, 'Something of (the poet's) interests as a writer becomes evident if we look at a short extract from (title of a poem).' You then need to find a suitable quotation, which, ideally, should be no more than four lines long. The reason for this is that you need to remember your reader: you cannot quote huge chunks from a poem or your reader's attention will wander. You need to provide him or her with just enough evidence so that he or she has a clear idea of what this poem is that you are going to talk about. How do you find a suitable quotation? Well, the earlier chapters of this book should have shown you how to choose a suitable passage: what you are looking for is a passage that conveys fairly clearly some of the concerns at the heart of the author's work. If you quote four lines, try to discuss them for eight lines. Similarly, if you quote two lines, discuss them for four lines. A vital rule of essay-writing is that **if you quote you must analyse what you quote**: the meaning and significance of a passage are never self-evident. Indeed, your reader might be tempted to interpret the quotation in a different way from you, so you need to step in smartly after a quotation and establish your sense of what is important in the extract. What happens when you do this is that you are beginning to establish a view of the writer from the evidence of the text.

One way of thinking about a paragraph is to see it as **a text–analysis–conclusion sequence**. Let me explain what I mean by this. You introduce a section of a poem, and then discuss it, but at the end of the paragraph you must pull the threads together and spell out what you have proved so far. It might be a very modest conclusion. For example, if you were writing about Wordsworth you might, at the end of your second paragraph, conclude that it can be seen that he writes about nature, but, by the very fact of spelling out what you have established so far, your argument has got under way. What your **third paragraph** will essentially be dealing with is what more can be said about the poet, and, as each paragraph asks this same question again, a fuller and more complex picture of the writer will develop. This is a way of making sure that an argument develops in your essay: the method is to write in substantial paragraphs of roughly equal length, summing up what you have established at the end of each paragraph so that a consistently more complex sense of the poet develops. The third paragraph of your essay, therefore, should repeat the pattern of the second paragraph; an introductory sentence, a short quotation, discussion of the quotation, and then a conclusion. What you should find yourself saying in the conclusion to this paragraph is more or less this: 'Previously I established A, now I have established B. When I put A and B together what I can now say about this writer is this . . . '. This method guarantees that you work from the evidence and also guarantees that you build an argument. An essential thing to tell yourself, is that you can prove a lot from a little. I have read far too many essays where students make a point and say that this can be seen in the following poems, and then produce a list of titles. Unfortunately, titles alone prove nothing. By contrast, a few lines from a poem provide you with all the evidence you need to support large ideas about a writer. But you must remember to spell out the larger point that you are establishing from the small, manageable piece of evidence.

As you go on to your **fourth and fifth paragraphs**, the pattern of the individual paragraphs can remain the same, but your overall case should be advancing as you turn to an extract, discuss the lines quoted, and then sum up the case so far. The reservation you might have is that this approach might seem too mechanical. Part of the answer to that criticism is that you don't need to stick rigidly to this pattern. There might well be paragraphs in an essay where you feel that a more general discussion is going to prove more useful than quoting an extract, and there might be paragraphs where you feel that you need to talk about, say, a range of images in several of the author's poems. The structure, therefore, can be fairly flexible, but whatever you do you should try to keep to paragraphs of roughly equal length, as this is the very best way of maintaining your control over your material and ensuring that your argument does actually advance. The other response to the accusation that this approach is too mechanical is to concede that it is, but it is much better to be systematic and well-organised in an essay than to be obscure and confused. More positively than that, however, the simple approach I am describing here might seem mechanical but it can help you write essays in which you build up a very complex sense of a writer. This is because it is an exploratory method: you start a paragraph with a quotation, but at the start of a paragraph you don't really know what conclusion you are going to reach. This is the opposite of the approach where you make a point and then refer to the text to back up your point: in that kind of essay you can only write down what you already know. The kind of method I am describing, however, allows the essay to work for you, encouraging you to venture along into areas you didn't expect to enter. It is vital, though, that you always sum up where you have got to at the end of a paragraph, so that you know that your next paragraph will have to advance upon the case you have established so far.

The result should be that a full and interesting answer develops as you advance from paragraph to paragraph. There is, however, one final complication that you might try to incorporate in an essay. It is a good move if you can give an essay a boost or change of direction about two-thirds of the way through. After about five paragraphs (one of introduction, and then four of discussion) the chances are that you will have mapped out a fairly clear sense of the writer's work. It is therefore a good idea to try to do something slightly different in the **last third of your essay**. How to achieve this redirection of an essay is something that I try to explain in the following sections on Yeats and Browning. This final change of direction is not, however, essential. An essay that steadily builds a coherent view of a writer is a good essay. At the end of an essay, of course, you need a **concluding paragraph** which spells out this final overall conclusion you have established. In some ways this should prove almost an embarrassment to write, because it can only reiterate the view that you have taken such care to build during the course of your essay. What you might discover, however, if your essay has worked well, is that you really enjoy writing this final paragraph. You might well be so pleased with the view of the writer that you have managed to put together that you find the words flow at the end as you confidently sum up your feelings about the writer and the question.

## W. B. Yeats

It all sounds so easy, doesn't it? An essay format that enables you to put together a controlled and confident answer to a question. No doubt, however, you have spotted the gap in my argument so far: I have described in detail the shape of an essay, but said very little about what precisely goes in each paragraph. It is very easy to say, 'Look at a quotation and then discuss it', but what exactly are you meant to say about each quotation? Well, to a large extent the earlier chapters of this book should have given you some ideas about what to say, for they have dealt with how to identify the central themes in a poet's work and then gone on to describe how you can discuss how a poet brings his themes to life. How to employ such an approach in an essay is, however, a slightly different matter, so it is to this that I turn now with a look at a question about W. B. Yeats. I hope it is clear, though, that what I say about an approach to Yeats should also work with any poet that you are required to write about.

The first step is to read and think about the questions set. Here are three questions about Yeats from examination papers:

1   Choose two or three of the following poems and show what qualities of style and content reveal Yeats to be their author: 'An Irish Airman Foresees his Death', 'Wild Swans at Coole', 'Easter 1916', 'A Prayer for my Daughter', 'Among School Children', 'Byzantium'.

2   'All Yeats's poetry derives its energy from the tension between obdurate reality on the one hand and imagination, memory or desire on the other.' Discuss, with reference to two or three of Yeats's poems.

3   'Ireland is Yeats's inspiration and subject matter.' To what extent is this true of the poems you have studied?

As is always the case with examination questions, all three of these questions look frightening. A moment's thought about any question, however, should be enough to see that it is raising standard issues about the poet and about poetry. The first question here, for example, the one about 'style and content', is a very straightforward question which asks you to discuss what Yeats writes about and how he writes about it. The second question, about his poetry deriving its energy from a tension in his work, is also straightforward: it directs you towards one way of expressing the central theme in his work, and in its reference to a tension asks you to discuss how he brings his theme to life. The third question, about Ireland, is rather different from the first two, however, because it asks you to focus on a more narrow topic. You would need to be very careful that you kept to the specified subject matter in your answer; what you would probably discover, however, is that, in the end, you were again discussing what Yeats writes about and how he writes about it. What I mean by this is that Yeats is obviously not just presenting us with a traveller's guide to Ireland. On the contrary, Ireland can be said to be the medium through which he will explore the large issues he explores in his poetry, and these large issues will be the issues that are explored by all poets. In some way his concern will be with a search for order, stability and meaning in a confusing world.

Most questions on poets, therefore, are essentially questions concerned with what the author writes about and how he writes about it. More often than not, it will be quite sufficient to refer to no more than three poems in your answer. Indeed, the question will often instruct you to limit yourself to two or three poems. This might seem to be a sacrifice of the large amount of work you have done on a selection of the author's poems, but it is not: the work you did on the whole range of an author's poems will indirectly feed into and strengthen what you are saying in your answer. If you decide to discuss three poems, the most sensible approach, after your introductory paragraph, is to devote two paragraphs to each of the poems in turn. The only danger in this approach, particularly if you are looking at short lyric poems, is that your answer might not amount to much more than three pieces of practical criticism loosely stitched together. But this can be avoided if you follow the advice I have given earlier, and which I try to demonstrate here, about how to build an argument.

The Yeats question I am going to take a look at here, in order to illustrate how larger questions about the poet and poetry underlie any particular question, is the most specific of the three, the Irish question. The question reads, '"Ireland is Yeats's inspiration and subject matter." To what extent is this true of the poems you have studied?' Remember that all an **opening paragraph** needs to do is set up the issue: it can start with superficial impressions of the writer, but end by holding out the promise that the essay as a whole will probe more deeply. the following paragraph would be quite sufficient:

> There are many of Yeats's poems that reveal that he is an Irish poet, perhaps most obviously those poems that make reference to Ireland in their titles. These include the three poems I am going to discuss in this essay, 'The Lake Isle of Innisfree', 'Easter 1916', which deals with the uprising of that year, and 'Sailing to Byzantium'. The exact role of Ireland in Yeats's work is, however, hard to define. It is not something that can be summed up easily but rather something that needs to be assessed from a close look at the evidence of his poems.

Can you see how this is a non-committed opening paragraph, which gently introduces the issue to your reader whilst holding out the promise that all will be revealed in the course of the essay?

Your **second paragraph** can start to explore the issue. What is again needed is a simple opening sentence that precedes the first quotation. For example, you might write, 'Some ideas about Yeats's attitudes to Ireland can be derived from an early poem, "The Lake Isle of Innisfree", where he writes about how he longs to escape from the city to Innisfree.' At this point you do not need to know what you are going to prove or discover in the essay. It might of course be the case that you do know the direction you are going to take, but you do not need to have everything worked out in advance. Because you are building an answer in paragraph units, you can build step by step, allowing an answer to evolve. You might start by quoting the first verse of 'Innisfree':

> I will arise and go now, and go to Innisfree,
> And a small cabin build there, of clay and wattles made:
> Nine bean-rows will I have there, a hive for the honey-bee,
> And live alone in the bee-loud glade.

I have suggested throughout this book that you start by looking for a tension: the implicit tension here, I feel, is between the reality of the everyday world and the simplicity of Innisfree. This opening impression of Innisfree is idyllic and harmonious: this is apparent in the lazy, reverie-like feel of the lines as if all the abrasiveness of life has been left behind. The images create a picture of an idyllic rural retreat. Everything is simple yet self-sufficient: the poet will make his own home, and feed himself on vegetables and honey. A very precise sense of this vision comes across, for example in the way that he envisages it down to the detail of 'nine bean-rows'. I have discussed this passage, but now I need to say where this leads me. I need to make a larger statement about what I have established so far. At this early stage of the essay I don't need to draw any kind of ambitious conclusion: it is sufficient to state, for example, that it is clear that Yeat does draw his inspiration from Ireland and that in particular he seems to have a fondness for the traditional and rural Ireland.

This becomes even more apparent as the poem continues. The **third paragraph** in the essay might now therefore turn to these lines:

> I will arise and go now, for always night and day
> I hear lake water lapping with low sounds by the shore;
> While I stand on the roadway, or on the pavement grey,
> I hear it in the deep heart's core.

Yeats effectively and economically draws a distinction between the city and the isle of Innisfree. A sense of the city is conveyed in the one line about the roadway and pavements: Yeats uses the word 'grey', and it does seem a depressing picture of a dull and colourless life. This becomes even more apparent when we contrast the attractiveness of Innisfree, made vivid in the image of the water lapping. It all seems to be summed up when he uses the image of the heart. It is as if he wants to escape to the heart and heartland of Ireland, which somehow seems more alive than life in a town. Now what can I conclude here? It is again the case that Ireland is central, and Ireland is certainly his inspiration, but is it his subject matter? Can you see how I am trying to take stock at the end of the paragraph, and using the words of the question to sort out my ideas? It is a process that I shall need to repeat at the end of each paragraph. What I feel here is perhaps his subject matter is not specifically Irish. The desire to escape from the harshness of modern life to a gentler way of life is a perennial theme in poetry rather than a specifically Irish theme. Yeats is therefore exploring an issue that poets have turned to time and time again, although his way of making this theme come to life is through thinking about Ireland.

Can you see how I have made a considerable advance in developing an argument, and have done so by working logically? I have avoided the problem so many people experience in writing essays of tying themselves up in knots. The whole secret is to work gradually from the evidence, pausing at the end of each paragraph to assess your progress in answering the question set. Now, as I start my **fourth paragraph**, I can turn to another poem. What might go wrong at this point is if I introduce a second poem too abruptly. This paragraph needs to take its lead from what I have just said at the end of the previous paragraph: I need a link in order that the essay will read coherently and hold together. If I had studied Yeats, I would probably know enough about his work to say something like this: '"The Lake of Innisfree" is, however, an early poem by Yeats in which the tension is not particularly complex. A more complicated attitude might well be apparent in "Easter 1916": this is not just because it is a later poem, but because it deals with the violence of civil unrest.' Can you see how gradual and steady my approach is? I am not making any large assertions about the poem in advance of looking at the evidence; I am making a reasonable guess about the fact that 'Easter 1916' should prove to be a more complex poem, but I am not presuming to offer an evaluation of the poem in advance of the evidence. What happens in 'Easter 1916' is that Yeats talks of the people he has met in Dublin streets: they are people he once scorned, but their deaths in the Easter rising have made them heroes and martyrs. It is a difficult poem, and could prove very confusing unless I focus on a few lines to try to work out some of the nuances of what Yeats is saying; in this extract he describes one of the rebels:

> A drunken, vainglorious lout.
> He had done most bitter wrong
> To some who are near my heart,
> Yet I number him in the song . . . .

Here was a man who offended the poet's moral standards with his drunken and loutish behaviour, and in addition offended the poet personally because of his behaviour towards Yeats's friends or relatives. Yeats is now, however, confused and in doubt, because this man who seemed so awful has become a hero. At times, such as here, it might prove necessary to introduce additional lines from the poem to help explain and explore the point. Yeats writes of what has happened to the man:

> He, too, has been changed in his turn,
> Transformed utterly:
> A terrible beauty is born.

This might seem hard to understand, but it isn't if we apply our usual ideas about order and disorder in poetry. The point is that the rebels, including this drunken lout, disrupt both the calm of Ireland and the civilised calm of Yeats's mind, but there is something inspiring about their actions that makes them fit subjects for celebration in verse: what they embody is heroism and the promise of a new dawn of freedom for Ireland. They suggest a new order, an order that overturns the kind of aloof civilised order that Yeats has clung on to. When Yeats talks of a 'terrible beauty', therefore, it is something contradictory that is being conveyed, for it is violence and disorder that is none the less romantic and glorious, for it rises so spectacularly above the rut of conventional prejudices and convictions. The conclusion which I draw from all this is that Ireland is again at the centre of Yeats's poem, but, as with 'Innisfree', I feel that, although Ireland has provided the inspiration, Yeats is writing about universal issues – in particular, in this poem, the possibility of creating a new social order. But it is the Irish context that makes the poem real and immediate.

Where I can advance from here, in my **fifth paragraph**, can only be determined after I have found another section of the poem to discuss. These lines about the dead rebels caught my attention:

> We know their dream; enough
> To know they dreamed and are dead;
> And what if excess of love
> Bewildered them till they died?

Yeats is asking himself difficult questions. He is puzzled about the significance of their deaths: it is love of Ireland that has driven these rebels on, but love of Ireland has resulted in their own deaths. This is glorious, but is must be wrong in some way. Can a new civilisation and freedom result from something as uncivilised as bloodshed and death? The poem is, therefore, not just a straightforward hymn of praise to the dead, but an agonised exploration of what we are to make of these deaths. I think it is clear that the poem could not have been written without the pressure of events in Ireland that disturbed and worried Yeats, but, at the same time, as the presence of the words 'love' and 'death' in these lines indicates, the subject matter is more universal: Yeats is asking what order if any can replace the reality that we are born into. Whereas in 'Innisfree' there is a simple escape to an idyllic island, here there is a more contradictory examination of what political hopes and aspirations amount to. My feeling, therefore, is that the poem starts with events in Ireland, but becomes a more universal consideration of the complex realities of political and social life. So much of the power of the poem, however, comes from the fact that it is real events and real people that Yeats is using to explore a theme which we can see is relevant in settings other than Ireland.

It is now time to move forward to my **sixth paragraph**. In a way I have already answered the question set: I have shown that Ireland is Yeats's inspiration but suggested that his subjects are those subjects that have exercised the minds of all poets at all times. I have tried to show how he deals with the harshness and problems of the real world whilst also introducing the dream or desire of a simpler or more ordered existence. 'Easter 1916', in particular, is the kind of poem that throws us back onto all the contradictions and difficulties of existence, although it never sacrifices a dream of a new order. Having established this, what I now want to try to do in the last third of my answer is change course in some way. As I have already said earlier in this chapter, the last third of an essay does not need to change direction. It is quite sufficient to keep on steadily building a coherent case, but there will be times when, having mapped out the issues, a new emphasis seems necessary or appropriate in the last section of an essay. The way to achieve this with any writer is more or less the same. The first two thirds of your essay should have established a clear sense of the themes and tensions in his or her work; the last third of an essay can concentrate more on showing just how complicated the tensions are in one of the writer's poems. The result is that you can conclude your essay with a convincing demonstration of the poet's complexity: two thirds of your essay has sorted out an impression of what the poet writes about and how he or she writes about it; the last third can lay more stress on just how complicated the poet can be.

If that is too abstract, what I mean might become clearer as I turn to 'Sailing to Byzantium'. At the start of this poem Yeats seems to turn his back on Ireland:

> That is no country for old men. The young
> In one another's arms, birds in the trees
> – Those dying generations – at their song . . . .

It is as if he wants no more to do with Ireland, and has come, in his imagination, to the holy city of Byzantium. This is again, therefore, a poem where the poet turns his back on reality and dreams of escape. As in the other poems we have considered, we can conclude at this stage that it starts with Ireland but soon expands into exploration of a perennial and universal theme of poetry, in particular the dream of escape. He wants to escape from a world where people grow old and die, and so imagines himself as the court poet of Byzantium who will

> Sing
> To lords and ladies of Byzantium
> Of what is past, or passing, or to come.

At first glance this might seem to express a very simple desire to escape from the real world, but I think a more complex picture emerges if we think about the implications of this role that he envisages for himself: he has become a sort of court gossip, commenting on the lives of the Byzantine aristocracy.

The lines I have just quoted conclude the poem, and, when we sense the absurdity of this new role, we might well return, in the **seventh paragraph**, to take a closer look at the opening stanza's evocation of Ireland:

> The salmon-falls, the mackerel-crowded seas,
> Fish, flesh, or fowl, commend all summer long
> Whatever is begotten, born and dies.
> Caught in that sensual music all neglect
> Monuments of unageing intellect.

Initially Yeats seemed to despise everything about Ireland, and these lines again harp on death and the physical process of ageing. But what now perhaps becomes more apparent is the teeming sense of life in this opening stanza, conveyed in the rich and abundant imagery of this stanza. It is as if, at a surface level, the poem embraces escape, but escape comes to seem shallow and even tawdry and so the poet throws himself back onto life. It is the kind of tension that we encounter in much of the finest poetry: the poet does not force a concept of order upon us, but turns back to the disorder of life. He seems ready to accept all the diversity and confusion and complexity of life, and, in this poem, even to celebrate it. In terms of the question I am answering, the **conclusion** I can draw is that Ireland again provides Yeats with his inspiration but that, as always, he soon expands into a more universal theme. In the end, however, he always seems to come back to Ireland, just as in this poem he seems finally to reject Byzantium for the complex reality of Ireland. This is the conclusion I can draw, but what I have also been trying to show is how an essay can slightly change direction at the end. I haven't redirected my argument here, but what I have tried to do is focus rather more directly on the brilliance of this poem. And really this is the kind of adjustment that it is possible to make in the last third of an essay: the first two-thirds of the essay can be devoted to mapping out a sense of what the poet writes about and how he writes about it, but once you have established this you can, in the last third, concentrate rather more directly on just how well he writes. If an essay is organised in this way you have really spent two-thirds of your space showing your understanding of the poet and a third of your space expressing rather more directly your appreciation of the writer and his work.

## Robert Browning

Yeats is one of the most difficult poets, and it might therefore be the case that the details of analysis in the section above could have obscured the points I am trying to make about how you can tackle a question on any poet. For this reason I now want to provide a further outline illustration of an essay answer, but this time I shall try to keep everything as simple as possible. The poet I am going to discuss is Robert Browning, but I shall try to avoid any undue complications. As far as is practical, I shall just concentrate on the method of an answer, a method which, in fact, is exactly the same as that I employed with Yeats.

Here are three typical examination questions on Browning:

1  'So many utterances of so many imaginary persons, not mine.' Discuss three poems in the light of Browning's warning.
2  What aspects of love seem to you most effectively portrayed in *Men and Women*?
3  Discuss three of Browning's poems that show the variety of his achievement.

It is again the case that all the questions are essentially asking you to consider what Browning writes about and how he writes about it. In each instance you need refer to no more than three of his poems. The question I shall tackle is the third one, about the variety of his achievement.

**Paragraph 1.** The first paragraph sets up the issue. You don't need to provide an answer yet; indeed, how can you indicate the variety of Browning's achievement before looking closely at the poems that will illustrate this variety? Start with a fairly general comment on the author, but at the end of the paragraph hold out the promise that your essay as a whole will conduct a thorough exploration of the nature of his work. With Browning, you might start by saying that it is apparent that he is a lively and energetic author, and that there is obviously a certain kind of variety in his work, as *Men and Women* consists of a series of monologues from a wide range of characters who talk about their lives. Indeed, at first it is difficult to see any common thread in the poems, and it is therefore necessary to start by establishing some sense of what his poems have in common before considering their variety. Can you see the strategy of such an opening paragraph? A few, broad comments about the writer gently introduces the topic to your reader, but your reader is also promised that if he or she perseveres with the essay then he or she will finally be rewarded with a full and coherent sense of Browning's achievement.

**Paragraph 2.** It is often a good idea to start with a relatively simple poem by the author, as the themes that are central in his or her work are likely to be apparent here in a way that can be discussed confidently in the opening stages of an essay. I shall start, therefore, with 'My Last Duchess': this is a poem in which the speaker, the Duke of Ferrara, shows a visitor round his house. The visitor is a representative of the young woman that the Duke hopes to marry. The Duke shows the visitor the portrait of, and speaks about, his former wife, who is now dead. Rather than talk in general terms, provide a short quotation as soon as possible. This second paragraph might therefore start as follows:

> Browning's preoccupations as a poet can be seen in his early poem 'My Last Duchess'. In the following extract the speaker in the poem, the Duke of Ferrara, talks about his late wife:
>
> >          She had
> > A heart – how shall I say? – too soon made glad,
> > Too easily impressed; she liked whate'er
> > She looked on, and her looks went everywhere.

Taken out of context these lines might seem baffling, but by the time you come to write an essay or examination answer on Browning you should be familiar enough with his poetry to start working from this small amount of evidence. But, even if you didn't know anything about Browning's poetry, the idea of order *versus* disorder should help you interpret these (or any) lines: what is being hinted at in these lines is the Duke's distaste for his wife's freedom. She seemed to be indiscriminate in her feelings and affections, and it is clear that the Duke did not like this. In the casual aside of 'how shall I say?' Browning manages to convey a sense of a fussy, pedantic man, a man who chooses his words carefully, whereas his wife was impulsive. At this point you need to sum up what you have established so far. You might feel that you have made little progress, but however modest your conclusion it is essential that you write it down. For example, it would be quite enough to say that an impression of two very different personalities has started to emerge in the poem.

**Paragraph 3.** A look at another extract will help you flesh out this first impression and enable you to push your argument forward. In this section the Duke is again talking about his wife:

> Oh sir, she smiled, no doubt,
> Whene'er I passed her; but who passed without
> Much the same smile? This grew; I gave commands;
> Then all smiles stopped together. There she stands
> As if alive.

The Duke's anger at his wife's behaviour is again apparent here. Yet I don't get an impression of his wife being at fault; on the contrary the Duke seems authoritarian and life-denying. Indeed he seems happier with the portrait of his wife, 'as if alive', than he was with her when she was alive. What this leads to is a sense of a man who wants a life ordered in his kind of way. The poem is a dramatic monologue, and what it seems to offer is one speaker trying to hold together his view of the world and how things should be. It is possible to conjecture that all the monologues have this in common: that Browning returns again and again to speakers who offer their own view of the world, and their own way of organising the world. The Duke, certainly, is a man who tries to order a disordered world and wants everybody and everything to fit in with his requirements.

**Paragraph 4.** I have started to establish a sense of a possible pattern that runs through Browning's verse. What he seems to write about is how one speaker orders his sense of the world, and his way of writing about this seems to be through the dramatic monologue, where we can see and judge the speaker in the poem. The pattern will vary in other authors, of course, but by this stage of an essay you should feel that you have started to pin down some sense of the themes that the poet writes about and some sense of how he writes about them. Now, in a fourth paragraph, you can proceed to fill out this initial impression. In the case of Browning, an appropriate poem to look at here would be 'Andrea del Sarto' (although dozens of other poems could be introduced just as effectively at this stage of the argument). If you have read 'Andrea del Sarto' you will know enough to say that

> Another speaker with shortcomings in his personality features in 'Andrea del Sarto'. There is again tension between the speaker and his wife, although on this occasion the wife is alive. The tension is apparent in the opening lines of the poem:
>
> > But do not let us quarrel any more.
> > No, my Lucrezia; bear with me for once:
> > Sit down and all shall happen as you wish.
> > You turn your face, but does it bring your heart?

Here is another speaker who wants life to be quiet and well-ordered, but this time the impression that comes across is pathetic rather than bullying. Andrea del Sarto seems to be pleading with his wife. The conclusion you might draw is that we can see the consistency of Browning's theme, how he again turns to one character who wants an ordered and organised life, but also how this poem is different from 'My Last Duchess'. The question has asked you to discuss Browning's 'variety'; one response to such a question is to show how he varies his central theme as he dramatises different kinds of personalities ordering their lives.

**Paragraph 5.** Each paragraph of our essay needs to build and advance the case. At this point, therefore, you would need to look at a further section from the poem, hoping to establish more. I have chosen a few lines from towards the end of the poem, where Andrea del Sarto dreams that perhaps in heaven he will get a second chance to make a success of his life.

> In heaven, perhaps, new chances, one more chance –
> Four great walls in the New Jerusalem,
> Meted on each side by the angel's reed,
> For Leonard, Rafael, Angelo and me
> To cover – the three first without a wife . . . .

Andrea del Sarto feels that he has failed both in his marriage and in his profession as an artist. There is something pathetic about this vision of making a fresh start in heaven. One way in which this comes across is in a tension in the imagery that runs throughout Browning's poetry. In 'My Last Duchess' the Duke is associated with images of restriction, whereas his wife is presented as moving about freely. It is the same in this poem: Lucrezia moves about freely, and seems to evade del Sarto's clutch and control, just as genius as a painter is beyond his grasp. And in the way he imagines heaven it appears that he can only think of it in terms of a restricted room with four walls. The impression that comes across is therefore pathetic but also sad. Yet there is also something rather mean-spirited about the whole thing as we see him once more, in the last line of this extract, complaining about his wife. The conclusion that can be drawn from all this is, I think, that the variety which exists in Browning's poetry is largely a matter of subtlety of characterisation, and of subtle distinctions between the speakers in the different monologues. The Duke of Ferrara and Andrea del Sarto are both men who try to cope with and structure their different worlds, but they are very different, and in a later poem such as 'Andrea del Sarto' Browning seems able to convey a very complex sense of human nature. Can you see again how I have tried to move the argument forward, extrapolating a conclusion from the small example of the evidence I have examined, but also trying to piece together all my ideas and impressions so far?

**Paragraph 6.** At this stage you might just want to continue building steadily, turning to another poem to show again how Browning's central theme remains consistent but how there is also tremendous variety in how he develops his material in individual poems. Another approach, however, if you felt that you had established a sufficient understanding of Browning's poetry by this stage, would be to turn more directly to an appreciation of one of his poems in order to demonstrate the force and complexity of his achievement. This is what I intend to do here, mainly because I want to say something, however brief, about a marvellous love poem by Browning called 'Two in the Campagna'. The speaker in the poem is talking about love:

> I wonder do you feel today
>   As I have felt since, hand in hand,
> We sat down on the grass, to stray
>   In spirit better through the land,
> This morn of Rome and May?

The speaker is trying to capture and understand the feeling of love. This opening stanza twists and turns, and is a twisting, complex question. In a very effective way this conveys the contortions the speaker's mind has to go through in trying to understand love. The poem seems consistent with what we have seen of Browning so far in that the speaker is trying to order and understand experience, but this seems far more positive than the other two poems. Andrea del Sarto seemed to regard himself as one of life's victims, but this poem offers an attractive and energetic grappling with experience. Can you see how those statements add to our overall sense of Browning's variety as a poet, because a thematic consistency has again been observed yet at the same time I have found myself commenting on how this poem differs from the two considered so far?

**Paragraph 7.** But what I really want to do in this last third of my essay is simply celebrate Browning's achievement. I feel that I have already established a sense of what he writes about and the fact that he can write about it with a great deal of variety, so now I want to concentrate on just how well he writes. As always, assertions in advance of the evidence will be of no value. I need to select a passage and then show how good it is. Consider this stanza:

> No. I yearn upward, touch you close,
>   Then stand away. I kiss your cheek,
> Catch your soul's warmth, – I pluck the rose
>   And love it more than tongue can speak –
> Then the good minute goes.

The central concern of this stanza is trying to capture the essence of a very special moment when the two lovers seem in complete communion. What makes it so brilliant is the ephemeral nature of that moment as they come together fleetingly. It starts negatively, then they touch, but immediately he stands away. The exquisite moment has been anticipated here, and then is achieved as he catches the woman's 'soul warmth'. But the experience is transitory. By the end of the stanza they are separate again. There is a startling quickness and agility about the movements of Browning's sentence as those movements are enacted. And this is something that is in evidence everywhere in Browning's poetry, as we see agile sentences twisting, turning, grappling to capture a sense of the world. The same effort to use language to order and understand the world is seen in the imagery here. He uses the image of the rose to try to convey what he means, but the very fact of plucking the rose seems to suggest a kind of aggression which somehow will destroy the moment. What Browning is saying is also suggested in the idea of loving 'more than tongue can speak': that in fact says it all. The feeling of love is beyond words, no 'tongue can speak' that feeling, but what we see in this stanza, and in the poem as a whole, is

Browning grappling with the problem of trying to express that feeling. In reading this stanza, and in reading the poem as a whole, there is a sense of everything almost falling apart, of Browning only holding the poem together by the most tremendous dexterity in the manipulation of words. That is, however, the essential quality of all great poetry, that we feel the poet establishing a precarious order: the poet tantalises us with a sense of completeness and coherence, but his poem is fluid and open enough to suggest the complexity and mystery of life.

**Paragraph 8.** The last paragraph of an essay can and should be fairly brief. It is where you sum up and make a final statement about what you feel you have proved. Do not make the mistake of introducing new material of further ideas in this last paragraph: it should simply be a pulling-together or all the threads that you have laid in the course of your essay. As I have said above, if your essay has worked well – and there is no logical reason why it should not if you follow the moves I have described – you should find yourself writing with confidence and enjoyment. And that, in a sense, is what I hope you have gained from this book as a whole – the confidence to enjoy, and to write about, poetry.

# Further reading

I HOPE it is clear by now that the best way of learning about a poet is to read and reread his or her work. At some stage you should read a broad selection of the author's poems, but it is sensible to concentrate on perhaps a dozen poems at the most; the more you read them the better you will understand them, and gradually you will come to grasp for yourself the essence or nature of the author's work. The value of repeatedly rereading a poem might seem doubtful, and certainly there are many students who feel they are much better occupied making notes from critics. Such students, however, are misguided. If you sit down and read the author you are studying for half an hour a day, you will soon gain a feel for the poems in a way that you will never acquire from any critical book.

So, reading the poems themselves is of supreme importance. It is always apparent to an examiner if a student hasn't read, or hasn't read sufficiently, the works he or she is studying. In contrast, the answers of students who have made a determined effort to read and become familiar with an author's works exude confidence in their references to the texts. And you can't bluff your way through this: there really is no substitute for reading and rereading. If you do turn to critics, work out why you are turning to a critical book. What is it that you hope to learn? Don't read critical books just because everybody else seems to be doing so. Identify what you want to get out of criticism, and choose your critical book accordingly.

You might, for example, want to find out more about the techniques a writer employs. In particular, you might want to learn about metre and rhythm. Two books which can help are G. S. Fraser, *Metre, Rhyme and Free Verse* (Methuen) and Philip Davies Roberts, *How Poetry Works* (Penguin). The second of these is a general introduction to poetry which approaches the subject from exactly the opposite direction from this book. I start with the search for theme and significance; Roberts starts with the sound and rhythm of poetry. If you feel that my book has neglected certain matters, Roberts's book can be relied on to deal with those topics. A further book worth mentioning here is Geoffrey Leech's *A Linguistic Guide to English Poetry* (Longman), which provides a comprehensive guide to poetic technique.

Another way of approaching a poem is from a consideration of the kind of poem it is, such as a sonnet or a ballad. A series of brief, very readable books published by Methuen under the general title *The Critical Idiom* includes volumes on all the major modes. (Fraser's book on metre is also in this series.) Some examples are John Jump's *The Ode*, John Fuller's *The Sonnet* and Paul Merchant's *The Epic*. Several other books in this series, such as Terence Hawkes's *Metaphor*, are also well worth consulting.

The books I have mentioned so far are primarily technical in their emphasis. You might, however, want to find out more about the age in which your author lived. A series which deals comprehensively with literary background is Longman's *Literature in English* series. A volume such as J. R. Watson's *English Poetry of the Romantic Period 1789–1830* contains the kind of information that you need to become familiar with if you are studying a Romantic poet. There are many similar guides which provide an interesting discussion of literature in its historical context and which may be available in your library. It helps if you know that such books are usually grouped together at the beginning of the English Literature section in a library. If, for example, you are studying Pope, don't just look up Pope in the catalogue but also go back to the start of the English Literature section, where you might well find a surprising number of relevant and interesting books.

The kind of books mentioned so far, which deal with poetic technique and background, are those which should prove most useful in complementing your reading of a poet. You might, though, feel the need to read books that deal more directly and comprehensively with the author you are studying. Don't however, make the mistake of using such books as a substitute for thinking; try to delay reading them until you have worked out your response. Such books can then serve a very useful purpose in helping you to extend your ideas. Again, don't read every book about an author that you can find; remember that time could be more usefully spent actually reading the author. The most helpful books on a single author are either collections of essays or short introductions to the poet. The Macmillan Casebooks – for example, the selection of essays on Tennyson, edited by John Dixon Hunt, and that on Donne, edited by Julian Lovelock – are very reliable books which provide you with a range of stimulating views from a range of critics. For a short introduction by a single critic I have often turned to the Arnold *Studies in English Literature* series: representative titles are *Wordsworth*, by John Danby, and *Pope's 'Dunciad'*, by Howard Erskine-Hill. If you want to read a longer book on a poet by a single critic, choose the most recent book, as the critic will often survey earlier discussions of the writer.

Another kind of book that can prove useful to the student of literature is a reference book. The established authoritative reference guide to poetry is *The Princeton Encyclopaedia of Poetry and Poetics* (Macmillan). It is an immense book which covers absolutely everything but can prove daunting to use. A far more modest reference book which you might find it helpful to consult is *Literary Terms and Criticism*, which is a volume in the Macmillan *How to Study Literature* series. And, finally, there are a small number of difficult but really stimulating books which deal with the whole subject of poetry, and make us think in a fresh way about both poetry and the criticism of poetry. The classic book of this kind is William Empson's *Seven Types of Ambiguity* (Hogarth Press). A more recent general book in this tradition which I have found very illuminating is Veronica Forrest-Thomson's *Poetic Artifice* (Manchester University Press). What is always particularly rewarding about such books is that, although difficult, they convey not only a sense of the complexity of poetry but also an acute sense of the pleasure to be derived from it.